GARAGE SALE ZEN

FURTHER ZEN RAMBLINGS FROM THE INTERNET

SCOTT SHAW

BUDDHA ROSE PUBLICATIONS

Garage Sale Zen

First Edition 2021

ISBN 10: 1-949251-45-4
ISBN 13: 978-1-949251-45-6

Library of Congress Control Number: 20718146094

10 9 8 7 6 5 4 3 2 1
Printed in the United States of America

GARAGE SALE ZEN

Introduction

Here it is, *The Scott Shaw Zen Blog 21.0,* originally presented on the *World Wide Web.* All of the writings presented in this book were written between August and November of 2021.

As was the case with the previously published volumes based upon *The Scott Shaw Zen Blog;* entitled: *Scribbles on the Restroom Wall, The Chronicles: Zen Ramblings from the Internet, Words in the Wind, Zen Mind Life Thoughts, The Zen of Life, Lies and Aberrant Reality, Apostrophe Zen, The Abstract Arsenal of Zen and the Psychology of Being, Zen and Again: The Metaphysical Philosophy of Psychology, Tempest in a Teapot and the Den of Zen, Buddha in the Looking Glass, Wo Ton' of the Blue Vision, Zen and the Psychology of the Spiritual Something, Pyrophoric Zen, Fragments of Paradox, Zen: Traversing the Entity of Non-Entity, Zen and the Ambient Echo: The Psychological Philosophy of Being, Paritical Zen and the Life Science of Becoming No Thing, Obscurist Occulto: Hiding from the Definition of Meaning, Principles of the Precepts, Left Turn at Reality Central,* and *Zen and the Outside of the Inside* this volume is presented exactly as it was viewed on *scottshaw.com* with no rewriting, punctuation, or typo corrections. From this, we hope you will receive the original reading experience.

This volume of internet ramblings is presented with the date and time listed as to when each blog was originally posted. Also, the blogs in this volume are presented from last to first. With this, we hope to present a transcendence back through time as opposed to an evolving evolution. In addition, we left out the traditional *Table of Contents* in an attempt to leave this volume with a much more free-flowing reading experience.

Okay, there's the information and the definitions. Read on… We hope you enjoy it. And, be sure to stayed tuned for the ongoing *Scott Shaw Zen Blog @ scottshaw.com.*

*   *   *

07/Nov/2021 06:53 AM

You can own a book but if you can't understand what the author is saying it's words possess no meaning.

No Reindeer Games for You

06/Nov/2021 09:03 AM

Everybody has the right to believe what they want to believe and do what they want with their own body and mind as long as that doing affects no one else. But, here's the problem, and this is where all life gets messy, what people do affects all kinds of everybody else, in all kinds of ways, yet people hold fast to their belief that they can do whatever it is they want, defined by whatever it is they are believing, in any given moment in time.

I believe this entire mindset has been brought very clearly into focus over the past, almost two years now, where the life of all of us on this planet has become entirely defined by the COVID-19 Coronavirus pandemic. People have wanted to behave the way they used to behave, doing the whatever it is they used to do, defined solely by what they thought about whatever. But, the problem has become that what you do can literally kill the person next to you.

...Last January (as I have explained in this blog in the past) my brother-in-law killed his mother by giving her COVID-19. He was out doing what he wanted to do, partying with his friends, someone gave COVID to him and he gave it to her. She died! He also gave it to his son who gave it to one of by brother-in-law's baby mommy's. But, they recovered. Though his son has been left with some lingering lung issues. This was all before the vaccines were available but the death was caused by one person deciding not to change their behavior and not take other people into consideration. From this mindset, he literally caused the death of someone. Think how many people have followed this same pathway of behavior throughout this pandemic.

There are sports stars who refuse to be vacationed, yet they want to play in their game. There are actors and musicians who refuse to get the jab, yet they wish to perform. There are workers, all across the spectrum of work, who refuse to get the shot, yet they wish to still go to their job. But, who are any of these people thinking about? Are they thinking about the person standing next to them that they may infect and possibly kill? No, they are holding fast to their own system of belief. But, their system of belief is not a proven fact. It is not proven to be God's Law. It's only their belief that they believe for whatever reason they believe it.

If you are not vaxed you can get tested today and be clear but have *The Rona* tomorrow. You can spread it. You can kill people. Due to the variants of the coronavirus that have emerged, it has been proven that the vaccines are not foolproof, but they are far better than no vax at all. That is fact. That is scientifically proven. From this, people should care enough about the All of Humanity to turn of their own personal whatever and get vaccinated. It keeps people alive! Yet, so many still fight the facts based in belief, pigheadedness, or whatever.

Now, this piece is not so much about the coronavirus and the vaccines as it is about the way people behave. I just use this pandemic as an example.

Think about it... In fact, think about your own life as you know you the best... How much thought do you put into thinking about your actions before you take those actions? How much thought do you put into thinking about how what you are going to do is going to affect someone/anyone else? The fact is, most people don't think about anyone else at all. The only time they do think about someone else is if there is something they want or can get from that person. And, this can be, *"Getting,"* on so many levels: love, hate, happiness, anger, lust, money, you name it... But, if it is not business, and I use that term, *"Business,"* very broadly, people don't think twice about how what they are doing will affect that person next to them.

Think about you... Think about the last time you took that other person out there into consideration. ...An individual that you do not know, you pass on the street, and you will never see again. Did you think about them at all if you did not want something from them? I doubt that you did. But, here lies the problem in all life. If you only think about yourself—if you only think about doing what you want and getting what you want and behaving the way you want then all of humanity, but you, is damned. Now, think how this spreads out across your society and the globe. Sure, you can think about you. Sure, you can talk about you. Sure, you can feel the way you feel, motivated by your self-induced whatever. Sure, you can do whatever it is you want, when you want, and not care about the consequences but by behaving like that all Life Chaos is set into motion.

Now, many will say, *"They can't babysit the whole world."* True. But, you can babysit you. You can choose to make what you do as conscience an action as possible. You can take anyone in your sphere of reality into consideration. You can care about them more than simply caring about yourself. From this, people won't be killing other people via unconscious behavior like giving them the coronavirus based upon some abstract system of belief that they believe they believe but can and will never be scientifically proven.

This pandemic will probably eventually be gone or at least become more manageable. But, this will never happen as long as people are locked into their own selfishness.

Think about the people that have hurt you as you have passed through your life—people that you did not even know. Think about the people that you have hurt that you did not even know. Because you didn't know them, that means that you may not have even known that you hurt them. But, does that make their pain any less real? Does it make your pain any less when someone hurts you that you do not know?

You can hurt people and never know. But, what is the instigation of that pain? You not being aware. You being locked into your own set of Life Definitions defined only by you.

Take a moment and step outside of yourself. Take a moment to think about someone else besides yourself. Take a moment to stop defining yourself only by what you believe. Take a moment to stop defining yourself simply by what you want. If you do this technique, even for a moment, more than likely you will encounter major new life realizations about you and how you interact with humanity. Perhaps you may even remove yourself from the *Consciousness of Selfishness.*

Be strong enough to choose to turn your own dogma off when it is for the betterment of all. If you do this, the world will become that much better. If everyone would do this, everything would become better.

Can you be strong and whole enough to not be controlled solely by the way you want things to be?

*   *   *

06/Nov/2021 07:20 AM

Practice feeling the feeling of feeling in love.

The Process in the Process and the Damage that Other People Do

04/Nov/2021 05:34 PM

As I told the story a month or so ago, some guy, in his junky old Ford pickup truck, sideswiped my car, killing it. I really liked that car! But, it is gone. The insurance company totaled it. They were great, however, they gave me the money right away. From that, I thought I was going to be able to get another car immediately. But, as I know I also told you all, due to the pandemic, the new car lots are empty and the cars they do have they are charging top dollar for. As for used car prices, the same, top dollar. So, I've been left in a quandary over these past maybe six weeks or so, where can I get a car???

Just today, we hopped in my lady's ride and headed the hundred miles or so down to San Diego. I saw a car on one of those car sites at a small dealership—a model that I always liked. CarFax claimed it had never been in an accident. I called the guy and he sang its praises. The price seemed right. So, we made the drive this AM. Man... Like I think I spoke about in yesterday's blog, *"Everybody lies..."* Now, I'm no mechanic but I do know a little bit about the what's what. The moment I walked up to the car it smelled like paint. It had just been painted! And obviously, due to the smell, with cheap paint. There were dents and scratches painted over. As well as a cheap job of bondo on the rear fin. All that drive time, all that gas, all that everything for nothing... All based on a lie.

Now, I know when and if you (I) buy a used car you are buying someone else's problems. They are most likely selling that car for a reason. Though they probably won't tell you what that reason is. Now, if you get that car for a good price and you have to put a few bucks into, AOK. But, if you pay top dollar... It's just not right!

So, here I am in the process. The process of the process. And, like so many things unleashed in and by this pandemic, we have all been left with less than ideal choices to make. Thanks China!

Back in the day, the 1980s into the 1990s, I used to own a bunch of cars all at one time. There were times when I had a couple of Porsches, maybe an MG or a Triumph, and, of course, my one or two main cars of stability, whatever that or those cars were at the time. My lady always reminds me that when I met her I owned five cars and a Harley-Davidson. Stupid! I know! But, that was the era of stupid. I guess I'm just paying the car-karma for all that ownership now.

Somewhere along the way, my mindset changed, however. I desired a more simple and frugal life and lifestyle. The cars feel away. Then, I was down to one. When and if I needed a new one, I would buy it. But, that was all in the before—the long ago and the far-far away. The before the world became defined by the pandemic.

So, I got thrown into all of this because some guy drove like shit and totaled my car. Unthinking and uncaring about the damage he unleashed. But, isn't that how most people are? Don't they do what they do, only thinking about themselves, and then they lie to cover up their tracks of responsibility?

You know, in Zen and other spiritual traditions, they always speak about, *"The Process."* That you really need to make The Process your tool. You really need to make The Process your ally. Sure, I get it. Make your pathway fun as un-fun as it may actually be. But, in some ways isn't that simply a Mind Fuck. Isn't that simply you playing a game with your own mind—trying to make things right when they actually are not?

So, here I sit, trying to figure it out. Trying to make The Process my friend. Trying to fix what some unthinkingly asshole did to my car and my life. ...As he drove a big piece of junky American Steel, his ride is still on the road. Mine gone to never-never-land forever.

If any of you people out there in internetland have any ideas about a fix for all/any of this, hit me up on Facebook or something. Let me know. If not, I guess I just have to keep dancing in The Process. Trying to find that right vehicle. ...Cause it's getting cold here in L.A. and I can't just ride my motorcycle through the winter. If I can borrow a line from GOT, *"Winter is coming."* Awh life??? ☺

The Truth of Publicity

03/Nov/2021 09:30 AM

As I have detailed in the past, whenever I teach a class on filmmaking, and I've taught a lot, I always begin by teaching the number one rule of filmmaking, *"Everybody Lies."* They lie about their production budget, their equipment, their actors, their crew, their distribution, you name it... Though I formulated this rule many-many years ago, in association with filmmaking, it truly has proven to the be the case of most people's lives. People lie. They lie for all kinds of no-reasons. Yet, they lie nonetheless. Thus, this rule has proven true for much of human reality.

...This is not cynicism. This is just the truth. The truth of the lie.

Why? I will leave that for other philosophers and other times. But, for the purpose of this piece, I will just leave it at that.

Often times we hear people speaking about (for example) film projects in the press. They detail this fact or that one. When the reporters say them, perhaps they believe what they are saying to be true. But, are they? And, when they are not, what responsibility does that reporter have to their listeners when they have spoken an untruth? And, shouldn't they have checked their facts better? Because if someone/anyone believes a lie, what are we left with?

I think to a couple of publicity campaigns that were launched. One of them fairly recently, regarding a film project, where what they were saying simply was not true.

In one, it was stated that, *"This was the first film ever shot entirely on an iPhone."* But, that was not true. I had shot an entire film on a iPhone a few years before the release of that film. Perhaps not as elaborate as the film being discussed, but filmed entirely on an iPhone nonetheless.

Going back a decade or so... There was this film that was released to theaters. They claimed it was the first film ever edited entirely on iMovie that was theatrically released. But, that was not true. Though I did the initial edit of the Zen Film, *Samurai Vampire Bikers from Hell* on time code decks, I had gone back and recut the movie in 2000 entirely on iMovie. That version was shown in theaters in Japan. This was at least a year before the release of the one claiming to be the first one ever edited on iMovie to hit theaters.

Now personally, I have never really called out the publicity based production factors that those filmmakers and/or distributors have chosen to call-up. I just did what I did. Art for art sake. Yet, there they were, claiming a something as something great and the first greatness of doing it but it was not true. So, they lied. And, I would imagine that, at least in terms of filming a movie on an iPhone, there were other filmmakers who did it as well before the proclamation of that one film.

So, what does all this leave us with? That's a good question? I think the main thing that you have to keep in mind as you pass through life and you hear things in the, *"Out there,"* is that you must take them all with a grain of salt. You must not immediately believe them simply because they are spoken. Because anybody can say anything, but does that make it the truth? No, it does not. Just keep that in mind. It may save you from a lot of turmoil when and if the truth of the truth is ever uncovered.

*   *   *

02/Nov/2021 03:59 PM

You can't undo what you've already done but you can choose to not associate with those people who judge you harshly for choices you previously made.

How Much Can You Care?
02/Nov/2021 09:24 AM

Have you ever been somewhere, perhaps in a public setting, and you hear two or more people speaking about someone they knew that passed away? You can hear the sadness in their voice and maybe you can even see the tears in their eyes. You can hear and understand their sadness but as you did not personally know the person they are speaking about you do not feel any deep emotion.

Has there ever been a time in your life when you were feeling very sad about something? Maybe someone you cared about died, maybe they were injured, maybe they just broke your heart—something happened that truly affected you but the people you discuss this something with don't really seem to understand your pain or even care. How does that make you feel?

This is one of the truths of life that very few people ever contemplate. Your pain is your pain but it is no one else's pain. Yes, in some cases more than simply you experience the pain but look to the person walking down the street next to you and they could care less.

Some people possess the capacity to understand and feel for the pain being experienced by others. How about you? Do you possess the capacity to feel and/or care about another person's pain? Or, are you simply locked into your own mind?

Do you pretend to care about the pain someone else is experiencing? Do you wish them well and say kind words to them, spoken softly?

Or, do you simply dismiss their feelings as you are not the one feeling those emotions? Think about this subject for a moment as it may provide you with some deep insight into the type of person that you have chosen to be.

When you feel pain, how do you want others to react to you? Do you want them to comfort you or do you simply want to be left alone in your emotion(s)? Each person is different and through life-schooling we each react to pain individually and in our own unique way.

Some people are very loud in their suffering. How about you? Some people are very silent in their anguish. How about you? Why do you behave in this manner? Do you ever ponder that question? Why are you who you are? Why do you behave the way you behave? And, how do you process your pain and the pain being experienced by others? Really, take a moment and think about this subject and define it in your own mind.

Sooner or later we each feel pain in our life. For some, we hope that someone else will care enough about us to care. Certain people even become angry when no one else cares about what they are feeling. Some take to the streets telling the world that they are hurting. Others jump to the defense of a person in pain as they have nothing more important to think about or feel. Again, who are you in this equation? How do you behave when there in pain in your sphere of reality?

The truth of life is, no one can feel your pain if they don't care about your pain. At best, we have people in our life who care enough about us, to care about what we feel. But, as in all things life, it all comes down to you. Who are you? Who's pain do your feel? Only yours? Or, do you care enough to experience what that someone else is experiencing? And, why do you wish to feel their pain? Moreover, who do you cause pain to? And, do you even care?

All life is life interaction. It is what you feel, equaling what you do. Can you care enough to not create the pain? Can you care enough to help others, even those you don't know, navigate through their pain? Or, is it all about you? When you are locked into the experience of pain is that all you think about? What about when someone else is feeling their own pain, do not have the capacity to even try to understand?

Ultimately, we will all pass through life's emotional journey. Sometimes that will equal loss and pain. How much can you care?

*   *   *

01/Nov/2021 03:21 PM

Right now, think about somebody you think about. Do something positive for them.

Don't just think about it. Actually do it.

How Many People Get Paid From Your Donations?

01/Nov/2021 10:06 AM

One of the big things about donating to charities that most people never think about is that the people who work for these charities get paid to do their job. Meaning, you and your donation is paying the salary of someone. No matter how seemingly worthy the charity you are donating to may be, the money you give is not only going to help whatever or whomever it is you are trying to help but it is paying for the lifestyle of the staff of that charity, as well.

In some cases, as has been well-proven, people take advantage of the giving of others to finance their lifestyle. In some cases, this is an elaborate lifestyle. For myself, having had a lot of opportunity to interact with the Korean-American community, who are by their nature very religions, (based in Christianity), I have personally witnessed how some of the ministers and the elders of a church are paid handsomely to do their job. This, while the constituency are far less well to do.

This is just one example. But, the fact of the fact is, it has very often been brought to public attention about how well a specific religious leader lives yet they prove to be far from holy in their personal actions.

Giving has long been taught to be a good thing. And, I personally highly agrees with this ideology. But, giving is most ideally done when you give to a specific person or persons or when you personally do something, very specific, that helps someone or something. Giving is best accomplished when you give to someone whom you know is receiving. From this, you know your giving is actually going to a direct source.

The problem with giving to a charity is, no matter what they claim to do; they pay people to do that whatever. The question you have to ask yourself is, are you willing to pay people to do that job? Sure, you may want to help whatever that specific charity represents, but are you willing to pay someone you do not know, will never know, and someone who may not even be doing their job with any sense of excellence, to live off of your money while claiming to be doing that whatever?

The people who do, the people who truly give to the greater good and contribute to the betterment of all can be seen doing their job. You know who they are and you can see what they are doing. For the most part, these are not the people who are asking you for your money. These are the people actually out there making things better.

So, think about these things the next time you watch a commercial on TV asking you for your donation. How much did it cost to make that commercial? How much did they pay the famous spokesperson to do that commercial? How much does it cost to broadcast that commercial that is asking for your money?

If someone is asking you for money there's a reason they're asking you for money. It's because they don't have enough money of their own.

Your money is your money; you can do with it whatever you want. But, before you give it to someone who is claiming to do something good with your money, question who is in the payroll line making their living off of your donation and are you willing to pay their rent and provide them with expendable income just because you see a commercial or hear a pitch calming that they will help that someone or that something out there if only you donate to their cause.

Things Left Unsaid

31/Oct/2021 07:02 AM

I was watching *The Sparks Brothers* documentary last night on Netflix. It is a very in-depth documentary into the life of Ronald and Russell Mael and their band, Sparks. Though it was a very comprehensive documentary, I could not help but notice how much was left untold.

Now, let me begin by stating, I was never really a fan of Sparks. This is not a criticism on any level as they were and are far more famous, rich, and successful than I ever was or ever will be. It was just that I never really liked the sing-songy nature of their music.

I think it's kind of interesting in that people of a younger generation than I probably don't even know who Sparks is. I think that is very common of those that come up through a certain era. If you weren't there, you weren't there and from this so much of that time and place is lost to future generations.

Though Sparks were around much before this, Sparks had a lot of commercial success in the 1980s. But, I remember long before that, in the 1970s and throughout the 1980s, I would see the two brothers standing in the back of L.A. nightclubs listening to the various bands of the era. Having been both born and having grown up in the L.A. area, they were and are truly a fixture of L.A. musical culture.

I think back to when I was early in my emersion in the film game. I used to be cast when the production needed someone with long blonde hair. As the years went on, I would say to my agent, *"I'm the last guy with long blonde hair in Hollywood..."* But, that's a whole other story. Anyway, in the early 1990s, I was on a set and I got to talking to this very pretty young girl. As it turned out, she was Russell Mael's girlfriend and she lived with him. I found that so interesting as I knew he was much older than I. And, I was in my early thirties. We had this long, joking conversation on the set about just how old he was as she didn't actually know. ...One of those stupid set banter things. As it turned out, she didn't really care. And, I get it, she was living with a Pop Star!

This brings me to a couple of points that I took away from the documentary. The second I will discuss in a moment that led to the title of this piece but the first was/is how when you come up with a certain elevated financial standing in life, you are truly presented with so many more opportunities. If you are a focused individual (or brothers) and follow your dream with dedication, while having that financial foundation, you can truly rise to great places. Most of us, like me, aren't like that. I always felt the impact of that fact on my life. But, the Sparks brothers grew up in the Palisades, here in L.A., which is an affluent community next to the ocean. Even though their father died when they were very young, as did mine, they were offered options that few of us will ever know. I believe it was, at least in part, those options that truly allowed them to follow their pathway of creativity onto success.

The second thing, as stated, led to the title of this piece. Though this was an in-depth documentary, there was so much left unsaid, like why did neither of the two bothers ever get married and/or have kids. I mean, in my life, I made a very conscious choice not to have children. As I semi-jokingly state, *"The nightmare ends with me."* I'm the direct end of two family lines. When I'm gone, and due to my age, that probably isn't too far off in the future, that will be it. The end. The family line(s) end with me. And, that's probably a good thing. But, there was really very little said in the doc as to what and why made the Mael Brothers live this seemingly very successful reality and not follow what may be called a more traditional family pathway. I mean, I get it, it's none of our business. It's not yours and it's not mine. But, if you're going to put a doc out there like that, it sets people to wondering. I mean, what broke off the relationship with the sweet little budding actress that I encountered all those years ago and Russell? Who knows?

But, all this discussion brings us to a bigger point... That point is, who really knows what about you and why? There are probably those that you tell at least some of your secrets to. But, most who know you, never really know you at all. There are those people like me, who are pretty much willing to spill my whole life out there to the world. But, most are not like that. And, even me, there are certain things that are none of your business. So, think about it... Who really knows the true you? Who really knows that inner you? And, if they were to make a documentary about you, what stories would you let the filmmakers tell and which ones would you keep locked deep inside of you?

*   *   *

30/Oct/2021 12:29 PM

Is your life defined by your successes or your mistakes?

*   *   *

29/Oct/2021 03:05 PM

If you are unhappy with where you find yourself in life. If you want something more but you don't quite know how to get it. Stop thinking about yourself for a moment, change your focus, and go out there and start doing things for others. You will be amazed at the life changing results.

It's All About What You Give

29/Oct/2021 07:31 AM

Recently, I've been writing a lot about the dynamics of human interaction. I've been discussing the human condition and some of my ideas about one's personal pathway to interaction. Now, I could sit down and discus the metaphysical aspects of Buddhism, Hinduism, or even Christianity with you forever but it doesn't seem that most people care about that. They want a pathway to a better life and maybe a few new ideas or tools that they can put into use to get to that better Life Place. Okay… Here they are: Give. Care. Do.

I know there are many people out there who spend their life giving. They follow a career path like a nurse or a doctor or a caregiver. They choose to make their entire life about the Give. And, that's great! We really need people like that who follow that life course. But, you don't have to have a degree to give. You can just be a giver.

Be honest with yourself right now… When you woke up this morning who did you think about giving to? Did you have any plan in place to do anything for anybody but yourself? If you did, great! If not, maybe it's time to re-think your life path.

Most people, as their pass through their days, are very self-orientated. They think about themselves. How about you? As you pass through your day, what is on your mind? Do you ever ponder this or do you just pass from one life experience onto the next?

Take a moment right now and really chart this out. What do you think about? What do you think about when you wake up in the morning? What did you think about yesterday? What were you thinking about just before you begin to read this blog? Does any of your common thinking think about what you are going to do for someone else in some positive giving manner?

The problem with giving is that a lot of people get giving confused with getting. As I've said in the past, many people give to get. Let's stop that. Let's take some time and give simply to give.

Okay, so how are you going to make this happen? What are you going to do today that is truly an act of giving?

I don't have the answer for that. That is something that you must come up with yourself. But, really do it. Really take today and give something to someone that they (not you) need.

You know, giving can become the commonality of your life. It can become your life mission. If it was, think how much better the life of everyone you gave to would become. And, if their life became better then wouldn't the entire world become just a little bit better?

It's easy to think about yourself. It's easy to fake give so you can get. But, take today, and maybe tomorrow, and maybe even the day after that, and really think to a grander scale of reality and give. Do something for someone else and make their life better even if in the smallest of ways. Do this and the all and the everything of everything becomes just a little bit better.

*　　　*　　　*

28/Oct/2021 06:53 PM

As long as you say you have something that someone else does not have there will be conflict.

Does Time Heal?
28/Oct/2021 03:13 PM

There is the old saying, *"Time heals all wounds."* There's other statements like that out there but they all come to seemingly the same conclusion, that through the passage of time you will no longer be hurt by what someone has done to you. But, is that true? Does the pain you feel, brought about by what someone else has done to you, ever truly go away?

Take a moment and think about your own life. That a moment and think about something someone did to you that truly hurt you. Is that pain actually gone? If it is, great! That's a good thing. But, I think for a lot of us, when someone hurts us, though we may learn how to cope with that pain through time, it never really leaves us.

In faiths like Christianity, the subject of, *"Forgiveness,"* is often discusses. It is taught that one should forgive those who hurt them. I guess that's a good ideology. But, I think it's kind of hard. When someone does something to hurt you, whether knowingly or not, you are the one left with the damage and the pain, they are not. So, who and why should you forgive?

I think one of the biggest problems in the subject of forgiveness, and the healing hands of time is that; the people who hurt you rarely own their participation in the hurt. They do what they do. They did what they did. They hurt you. Then, they are too lost in their own head to ever try to remedy the situation and to truly ask for forgiveness for what they have done that hurt your life and actually do something that undoes what they have done.

Think about the people who have hurt you. How many of them have actually asked for your forgiveness? How many of them of them have tried to right any wrong they enacted? My guess is, it would be very few if any.

The sad truth is, most people when they hurt someone hurt them because they don't care about them. If a person cared about you then they probably wouldn't hurt you. But, as they do not care about you, they do not care about the fact that you are a person with feelings, thus, they don't care if they hurt you. And, this is where many of the problems of life come into play. They are invoked by someone who does not care if they hurt you, me, or anyone else. All they have is the capacity to think about themselves. Many/most will deny any wrong doing in their hurting of others to the person, themselves, and to others. In fact, think about how many times someone has done something that hurt you and then they tried to turn that action around and blame you for what they did. Not right but that is what takes place a lot of times in life.

So, what can we do about this? I don't know? There is no obvious answer. But, the problem with allowing time to heal your wounds highly depends on how many times you have been hurt. The fact is, you may not have enough life-time available to emerge free from the pain.

Here's the thing, you must be the person to remedy all pain. If you have hurt someone, even if you have hurt someone you don't like, it must be up to you to repair that damage and heal that wound. Because if you don't, what does that say about you? Care enough to express your regret. Say you're sorry. Try to fix any damage you have created. For if you don't what does that make you?

Honestly, how much time have you spent attempting to repair any hurt you created even with someone you may not know, like, or care about? A better world begins with you. What are you going to do about it?

If you're the one on the receiving end, healing is a much harder question. I mean, people hurt people all the time. They hurt you, they hurt me. Some hurt anyone and everyone and they just don't care. That is not right, but that is life. So, what can you do? Some people pretend it doesn't hurt when it does. Some people are good pretenders. But, no matter how much you pretend, that hurt is not gone, at best it is simply locked deep down inside of you. All you can do to get past it is to try to find another focus—something that will take your mind off it. And then, hopefully, through time, the impact of that hurt may become less traumatic.

People shouldn't hurt people. There's no justifications or logic for hurting anyone; whether intentionally or not, for any reason. Never allow yourself to fall into the pattern of hurting one person or many people, because hurt only equals hurt. And, hurt, hurts.

So, try to live a good life. Try to steer clear of those who may hurt you. Never associate with those who knowingly hurt other people. If someone is personally hurting you, call them out, tell the world what they are doing. Maybe it will make them stop. But, when it comes down to hurting others, never do it. If you do hurt someone you must do all that you can to fix any pain you created. Because if you don't do it for them, who do you think will do it for you?

Stop the hurt!

*　　*　　*

28/Oct/2021 07:11 AM

If you had everything that you wanted would you have everything that you wanted?

*   *   *

27/Oct/2021 09:37 AM

Your life is not going to be remembered by how much you own but by how much you've given.

* * *

27/Oct/2021 09:35 AM

If you're stealing from one person to give to another all you are is a thief.

The Art of Un-Becoming

27/Oct/2021 07:44 AM

Most people pass through their life with very little change taking place. They decide who and what they are at a fairly young age and that is that. They do what they do, wear what they wear, eat what they eat, and they never allow any change or any evolution to take place. How about you? How much change has taken place in you in the past year, the past five years, the past decade, or more?

It is very common to know a person and then not see them for a number of years but when you do see them, those many years later, they still have the same hair style, they still wear the same style of clothing, they still listen to the same style of music, they still do exactly whatever it is they were doing way back in the way back when. Again, how about you? What are you doing different today from what you were doing ten years ago or more?

Life can be a process of learning and of evolution. It can be a process of change and gaining new awareness. It can be a grand ever-evolving story but few people allow it to be. Why? Because the known is known. The known is safe. But, by knowing all that you know, and knowing it for years-upon-years, what have you learned? What new have you experienced? How have you allowed yourself to feel that something new and that something different?

So, here's the thing, you already know what you know. Sure, you like what you like. But, why don't you give something new a try. Of course, it's your choice but you never know, you may find that you will love that something new, you just have to try it out.

Here's a few examples. Maybe change your hairstyle. If you're a man and you've always had short hair, let it grow out for a year or more. If you've never had a beard, grow one. If you've had a beard for a long time, shave it. If you're a woman who does her makeup everyday, stop. Go out with none. Go to the store and buy some new clothing in a totally different style than you normal wear. See/experience how the world treats you differently. Change your radio station. Listening to a different style of music from what you normally listen to. Even if you think you don't like that style of music, truly give it a try. Go to the bookstore (if any of those still exist) and buy a book about a subject you know nothing about. Read it. Learn. Try something different on the menu. Eat some food you've never had. Eat something (again) that you one time believed you didn't like. If you normally go to bed early, stay up late. If you usually stay up late, wake up a dawn. Stop thinking the same thoughts about the same things in the same manner as you normally think. That's a hard one but give it a try. Stop responding to people in the same way as you normally do. Say something different—behave differently toward them. Again, not easy, but change sometimes takes work. The thing is, change can be anything that changes you, but if you don't give it a try, you will never change, you will never evolve. Mainly, don't fight the different. Just experience it and learn from it.

Your life can be more. You can know more. You can be more. You can experience more. Or, you can just stay the same, live in that place where there is never any new evolution.

Give change a try. You may find an entirely different, new, and maybe even better you.

Favors from God
25/Oct/2021 08:00 AM

For anyone who believes that there is a greater being out there controlling this world, it is undoubted that they will pray to that being asking it for help. When they need something, when they want something, it is there that they will turn. For decades televangelists have sold the theory that if you live by the word of god, interpreted by them, that you too can get what you want: be successful, be healed, and get all that you want out of life. Think about it. How often do you pray to a greater being asking for guidance, help, or a way to get the things that you want?

The great Hindu Sage, Swami Sivananda wrote how when one is asking to get something to the powers beyond that they come into contact with the devis. The devis or goddesses are understood by Hindus to be demigods that, among other things, provide powers and gifts to us lowly people done here on Earth. Of course, the Hindu understanding of god and their gods is quite different from the One God ideology practiced in say Christianity, but to the believer it is no less real. If you want something and you either do not have it or can't seem to find a way to get it, you turn to the gods.

But, as Sivananda so aptly stated, once you bring these devis into your life, and they start providing for you, they will never leave and then you will find that there is a price to pay.

In true Buddhism, there is no god. Yes, there is the Buddha, but he is the idealized image of a man who reached the highest level of human consciousness. Though this pure understanding has evolved over the centuries and Buddhists now commonly pray to the Buddha, this is not an example of the true religion.

The reason I bring up Buddhism is that in this religion, which grew out of Hinduism, (the Buddha was a Hindu), it is taught that one should avoid desire at all cost. Though this is the true teaching, how few are the people that actually practice this advanced understanding? Few people have the mental capabilities to live a life focused on no desire. Thus, this brings us back to the practice that most people practice; that of praying to god to get what they want. Again, how often do you ask that greater power to help you to get what you want—whatever that want may be? I would assume that most of the people that read this blog, to at least some degree, reach out beyond themselves for that divine help, as this is a part of the human condition.

But now, think about this... What if no one had ever taught you that there was a god out there that you could turn to? Think about it, where did you first learn about god? For most, this theory was indoctrinated into them in childhood. Parents teach their children to pray. They do this via words and they do this via example. They talk about their beliefs that there is a god. They take their children to church where they are further indoctrinated into the belief of whatever is the belief of their culture. But, what if you were not schooled in any of this? What if you were never taught to ask god for a favor? What if you were never taught to believe in anyone but yourself? What if you were never fed and then re-fed the story, defined solely by the words of the teacher, that you can and should turn outside of yourself when you can't get what you want? Think how different your life and your life behavior would be.

Just as Sivananda explained that if one turns to the devis there is a life price to be extracted, think to all of those ministers and religious teachers who make their living by supposedly interpreting the words of god. They live this grand life while their flock do not. Yet, their flock pays them to tell them what they can do to hopefully get the small things that they want.

I always think to the South Korean Buddhist monks. If you ever encounter one, you will immediately know of what I speak. They wear the robes of a monk but they also all wear a gold Rolex watch. They're a monks but they wear a gold Rolex. Something just seems strange in all of that don't you think? Yet, it is an ideal example of those who teach the promise of god compared to those who live a life defined by hopes and dreams of wealth, health, success, and possessions. Who is selling what and why?

I could say, don't desire and you will be free. I could say, why pay people to provide you with a false pathway to god? I could say, let go of all of this god-stuff that you were taught and then you will come to a clearer understanding of who and what you truly are. But, who will listen? So, all I will leave with is think about how you came to your understanding of god. Who told it to you? Who sold it you? And, what if you did not believe in that something out there? Who would you be?

How would you be? And, what would you do the next time you wanted something and you did not know how to get it? If nothing else, your life, your mind, and your thought process would be a whole lot different.

Think about it...

* * *

25/Oct/2021 07:17 AM

What if life as you know it was just a maze that you had to get through to get out the other side?

* * *

25/Oct/2021 07:16 AM

If you know the next bite you were about to take was going to be your last bite how much would you appreciate it?

*   *   *

25/Oct/2021 07:14 AM

We are all going to die having not done something we wanted to do.

The less you want the less you will not have done.

*   *   *

24/Oct/2021 04:49 PM

If you can't do anything about it, you can't do anything about it.

*   *   *

24/Oct/2021 04:49 PM

If you can't find it, forget it.

*   *   *

24/Oct/2021 04:05 PM

Just because you stir a boiling pot does not make the temperature any cooler.

Taking Verses Giving
and Who is the Better Boxer
24/Oct/2021 07:53 AM

Once upon a time, in the long ago and the far-far away, if someone liked a band they would buy their record or their cassette or their CD, they would pay to see them perform, maybe they would even buy their tee-shirt or a poster of the band for their wall. If someone liked an actor they would pay to see their movie in the theater or buy a VHS or a DVD of the film(s) they were in. When someone liked an author they would purchase the book or books they wrote and read them cover-to-cover. If they liked an artist they would purchase one of their paintings or a print of that art work. Now/today, people do very little to support those they appreciate. They download their music from websites that pay the musical artist very little if anything. They watch the movies on streaming services or download them from illegal offshore sites that pay the actors and/or the filmmakers nothing for broadcasting their film. People download books from sites that give the authors nothing for their creative writing. Now/today people partake of the things they like: the music, the films, the art, the words, but they take and give nothing in return. Perhaps they saddest thing about all of this is that no one even thinks about this fact. They just take, they just consume, they just partake of what they like and they never think about the affect this will have upon the creative force that drove that whatever towards its creation. How about you? How often do you take but never give? How often do you ponder the question of, *"What do I give to those that I like what they have created?"*

We all understand the understanding of karma. Personally, I don't really like to use that word because it has become so cliché. This being said, that word is very descriptive of the process of life interaction. So, forgive me if I use it every now and then. But, the fact of the fact is, there is karma in all things life—there is karma in everything you do. Everything life has karma attached to it. But, no one wants to think about this. If something negative happens to someone else, they like to say, *"They got their karma."* But, if something bad happens to you, you get all upset and scream out, *"Why?"* No one ever wishes to look in the mirror. But, think about it, how much time do you spend actually contemplating how your actions are going to affect your tomorrow and how your actions are going to affect the tomorrow of someone else—particularly that someone else that you may like what they have created?

I get it, once a creation is created, it is out there in the Out There. It is available for the taking. But, here comes the difference and how that difference can and will affect your life. What do you about what you consume? How do you get it? What do you do with it? And, how do you repay the creator of that whatever, whatever that whatever may be?

If you are hungry, you will go to a grocery store and you will buy something to eat. There is an exchange of energy in all of that. The food growers and packagers get paid by the store to sell their products. The store stockers get paid to stock the groceries. The checkout people get paid to sell you the food. All has a balance of suchness. But, people take this process simply as the reality of eating. Very few think very much about it. They get hungry, they go to the store, they buy some groceries, and they go home and eat. It is all very expected. But, does that process of food buying cause you to think? Does it cause you to feel? Does it cause you to find your own inspiration? Most likely not. As it is not like the arts, it is not like the arts. But, how much time, how much energy, how much anything do you put into repaying and giving to the person who inspires you via their art: their music, their movies, their writing, their whatever?

The world has changed in recent years. The world always changes. But, the problem with/in the changes of the world in these recent years is that people have found a new way to become even more self-centered, (if that is even possible). They do this in how they consume. Sure, they like what they like. Sure, they like whom they like. But, no longer is there a need for any exchange. It has become all about the take.

So, think about this the next time you are listening to a song you like. Think about this the next time you are watching a movie or reading a book or looking at a piece of art you like. Question of yourself, what are you giving back to the person who created it? What are you giving them to let them know that you like or appreciate what they are doing? Remember, though it is easy to simply take in this current state of the world, should that be the definition of the world—should that be the definition of you?

You can take, you can consume, you can like what you like, you can love what you love, but if you do not give back to the creator of your likings, what does any of your liking or your loving actually mean? Are you only about the take? Or, are you willing to give for your taking?

Why You Give

22/Oct/2021 04:48 PM

I was doing a little of Spring Cleaning, here in the Autumn, and I donated a number of the amps I had to a local thrift store. I just wasn't using them. I mean, everything is so digital now that it is very rare that I even use an amp anymore. I just plug straight into my effects board and then into the computer.

Looking at those amps, I was forced to remember how grand it would have been if I had an amp or amps like that back when I was coming up. Back then, there was none of the modeling amps of today. None of the amps that are pre-filled with all kinds of effects. Me, I had to save and save until I could get enough money to buy just one effect pedal. Now, it's all in one amp.

Again, the amps weren't being used and I hoped to get them into the hands of someone who could make spectacular music with them. I hope by donating them to the thrift store that will open up the door of creativity for someone, where they can be purchased for a reasonable price.

Isn't that what giving is all about? Making someone's something just a little bit better?

Mostly, when I encounter people giving, they all seem to want something in return. They are rarely giving just to give. They give so that they will get. Get... Be that love, lust, fame, fortune, good karma, the sense that they are doing something good, or whatever. In some cases, they are giving just so the other person knows that they were given something and now they must repay the gift. It seems giving is rarely about the other person, it is all about the giver. How about you? When you give what do you give? Why do you give? Do you have a notion of receiving for your giving? Or, is your giving a wholly pure gesture? And, do you ever ponder any of this?

Keeping benefits no one except maybe yourself but if you give you open up a whole new world of possibilities for everyone.

*   *   *

22/Oct/2021 03:18 PM

Just because you wear a symbol of your faith does not mean that you are holy, blessed, protected, or saved.

Just because you pray does not mean that you are holy, blessed, protected, or saved.

Just because you proclaim your faith does not mean that you are holy, blessed, protected, or saved.

*   *   *

22/Oct/2021 07:18 AM

If all you want is one specific thing, why should you own anything else?

*   *   *

22/Oct/2021 07:10 AM

Have you ever noticed that the people who are the most opinionated hold opinions that no one should listen to?

The Status of Your Status

22/Oct/2021 07:09 AM

How do you feel about your life? How do you feel about you? How do you feel about where you have found yourself in life? How do you feel about your feelings and what you feel on a day-to-day basis?

In everybody's life, there are ups and there are downs. There are happy times and there are sad times. This is simply a condition of life. But, how do you feel on a daily basis? Are you happy, are you content, or are you frustrated, unhappy, and angry? Are you doing what you want to do; living the life that you hoped for? Or, are you in a constant state of frustration, agitation, anger, dissatisfaction, and unhappiness?

If you are dissatisfied, if you are unhappy, if your life is based in anger, what fault do you hold in all of this? Most people never look at the, *"Me Factor."* They never look at themselves. They simply prefer to look outwards. They simply prefer to blame that someone or that something else. That makes their unhappy everything so much easily to justify and explain.

Truly look at your life. Are you happy? If you are great! That means that you have done something right.

Truly look at your life. Are you unhappy? If you are, what caused you to arrive at this life placement? What did you do that caused you to arrive at a place of unhappiness and dissatisfaction?

If you cannot blame yourself, who else is actually to blame? Yes, some people do some very messed up things that hurt the life of others and they are wrong for doing those things. There is no doubt about that. But, if you choose to interact with that person who has driven you towards pain and unhappiness then aren't you at least partially to blame?

If you find yourself in a negative unhappy place in life, Right Now, take a long hard look at yourself. Do not focus your attention or your blame on anyone else. What did you do to arrive at this place in your life? What did you do to other people? What did you do to yourself? What choices have you made that cast you to this destiny?

If you are not happy, it is very-very important that you contemplate these questions and come to a very clear and definitive answer based on YOU. Because if you don't, if you don't look at and define your participation in the creation of where you find yourself in life, then nothing in your life will ever get any better.

Removing the Bad Element
AKA It's Not All About You

21/Oct/2021 09:01 AM

I had this one upside-down catfish in my aquarium... Well, I actually had two. Now, these guys are big. They are like eight inches long. The one was very docile. The other one aggressive, always chasing after the other upside-down catfish. I spoke about him (or her) in a blog not that long ago.

Anyway, I did a clean up and rearrange of the aquarium and the aggressive catfish just went nuts. All night I was hearing the splashing of him chasing after the other fish. I have long thought what to do about him as I liked him. But, by liking him I was allowing him to be a bully. I was enabling him. You should never enable a bully! I knew he had to go. Finally, I found this aquarium shop that would adopt him and now he is out of the aquarium. All is well with the world. No more splashing. Just everyone getting along.

You know, that upside-down catfish is a lot like the ways of the world. There are all these bullies out there. Maybe it is due to their size, maybe it is due to their voice, maybe it is due to their money, maybe it is due to their position of power, maybe it is due to their gang, maybe it is due to whatever, but they bully and they bully and they bully; truly hurting the life of one or more people and they get away with it until someone or something kicks them out of the mix.

I think we have all encountered people who have bullied others or ourselves via various methods as we have passed through life. It really suck, because while they are in our life/while they are in anybody's life, everything is not good, calm, happy, productive, and/or peaceful.

The problem is, how do we get them out? I guess that's one of the universal questions, because a lot of times, like my other upside-down catfish and the other fish in my aquarium, sometimes your are trapped in a space where you (personally) have no way out and no way to get them out. You want to be out, you want them out, but you don't know how to get out.

On a similar subject, I was in one of my local pet shops and there was this lady not wearing a protective mask. To put this is time perspective, right now, at least here in L.A. County, due to the coronavirus, it is required that all people wear masks indoors.

You know, for a moment, a few months deep, for those of us who were vaccinated, we felt free indoors as we were vaxed and felt protected from COVID-19. We didn't have to wear masks. Then came the Delta Variant and the vaccines, though still very effective, proved to not be one hundred percent protective against break-through cases. So, the masks came back on. I remember when this happened I was going into a Starbucks and this one lady was saying to her friend, *"I threw all my masks away."*

But, here's the thing, the mask is not so much to protect you, it is to protect the other person from you. You may have the coronavirus, not know it, and pass it on to someone else. But, there she was, that lady in the pet shop. Maybe she was vaxed, maybe she wasn't—an anti-vaxer; who knows? But, what she was doing was putting the life of other people at risk. Just like my upside-down catfish, she was only thinking about herself. But, it's not all about you. That is a very selfish perspective. Just like my big, bully catfish, there are many ways that people throw their assumed power around in an attempt to take and hold control and make themself feel all-powerful or all-something. Think how many ways people attempt to express his or her life opinion and in doing so hurt someone else. What if that lady spread the disease to someone in the pet shop and they died simply because she was not willing to do something so simple as wearing a mask?

We all have our opinions about this coronavirus pandemic. I've written about mine over the past year and a half or so in this blog. That's life. We all have our opinions. But, if you are not willing to take one for the team and do all you can to keep other people safe, what does that make you? Answer: A selfish bully. Because here and now even your breathing on another person could kill them. Get vaxed. Wear a mask. From this, maybe in the not too distant future we can get back to some semblance of normality.

So, what are we left with? We are left with the hopes that all of us have to live a healthily, happy, positive, productive, and non-attacked life. None of us want obstacles placed in our road by someone else. None of us want to be bullied by however that bulling may present itself.

What can we do? Not bully. Care. Care more about that other person that you do not even know. Care about them enough to do some small things like wearing a mask. It's not all about you! Wearing a mask is not that big of a deal.

Believe what you believe, that is your right. But, in all that you believe, care about that other person first. That is the only way to be an anti-bully.

*   *   *

20/Oct/2021 09:00 AM

When you make a mistake how much focused energy do you put in to trying to correct that mistake?

Do you attempt to fix and/or correct that mistake at all or do you simply live in denial and make excuses for creating that mistake?

Outside Anger

20/Oct/2021 08:23 AM

Though anger is an internal feeling, it is driven by external circumstances. If you feel anger, what are you feeling that anger towards? Think about it. Most likely it is focused on some external something; be it a person or a situation. That thing is out there but it is you that is feeling it inside of your being.

As you pass through life there will be those people or those situations that cause you to feel anger. The fact is, some people do things in order to get the feeling of anger to rise in someone else. It is their way of taking control over that person; whether they are conscious enough to realize that or not. There are also people who base their entire life upon finding something to be angry about. Anger is an intense, adrenaline filled feeling; it causes the blood to race and the blood pressure to rise. As it is an elevated feeling, some people become addicted to it.

If you look around at life, you will see anger is all over the place. Drive down any busy street and you will hear the horns honking, see the hand gestures, and view the clinched faces after just a few minutes. You don't have to look too far to see anger on the internet. There are people writing statements, there are protesting in the street, there are those people who create and churn up the anger in others for any number of reason but anger is a wholly internal process. If you allow it to enter you, and yes it is your choice if you allow it to enter or not, you may become controlled by it.

Think about something or someone you were angry at a year ago or maybe ten years ago. Do you still feel that anger. Most likely, though you may still not like that person or that situation, you no longer hold any anger towards them or it. Think about a time when somebody did something stupid while you were driving and it really caused anger to rise in you. Do you even remember that incident? Probably not.

Then, there is the other side of the anger issue, those times when your anger causes you to react and to do something. And, as that action is driven by anger, that action is most probably negative. It is done in order to lash out and/or hurt that someone or that something else that you are angry at.

Think about something you have done caused by anger. Did you hurt that person or thing you were angry at? If you did, what were the consequences to them/it and/or to you? Did doing that reactive something make anything any better or did it simply cause you to do something bad that set a whole new plethora of karma, created by you, into motion.

Most people never think about the reactive nature of the actions they take driven by anger. They just do. The problem with living life from this perspective is that you are not basing your life as defined by you. You are allowing that something *Out There* to cause you act and react. You are allowing that *Outside Something* to set your next set of life experiences into motion. And, in some case, what you do, based in anger, can cause a lot of badness to be brought into your life.

Some people feel empowered by the anger-filled actions they take. Some people feel empowered by causing others to become angry. But, in all cases of anger, if you are feeling anger, you are allowing some external something to take control over your mind and your emotions and control you and what you do. Is that how you wish to live your life?

Most/many people never attempt to control their anger. When they are lost in that moment of anger, it is all encompassing. But, it does not have to be that way. You can choose to control that emotion in you if you choose to. Do you choose to? Do you allow yourself to have the power of self-control to take control over your mind and not allow the doings of that someone/something else to take and hold control over your emotions and your motivation for your reactions?

Here's a simple practice: Next time you find yourself becoming angry, control it. Turn it off. Don't let yourself be angry. Certainly, do not let yourself do something reactive based on that anger. By doing this, you will witness the magic and the power of self-control you will encounter when you do not allow that external something to exercise more control over you than you have over yourself.

Most people never realize this fact... Most people never practice that fact... But, you do not have to be angry if you do not want to be angry. You can take the control away from that something outside of you and you can control you. Try it. You may be able to live an entirely better life, never controlled by that something outside of yourself.

* * *

20/Oct/2021 08:22 AM

How many excuses do you make?

*   *   *

20/Oct/2021 08:22 AM

How many lies have you told to get to where you are today?

Two Sides of the Same Story
18/Oct/2021 07:47 AM

There have been a number of people who have attempted to present the same story from two different points of view in novels and in film. For the novelist, this process is a bit more cumbersome and in my opinion not as easily consumed. In a film, however, you can see the two different points of view evolve in front of your eyes. First there is the story told from the perspective of one person and then the other.

Whenever you are living whatever it is you are living, that involves another person, do you ever take the time to realize and understand that the person you are living that life moment with may have a completely different understanding of that moment than yourself? I believe most people don't do this. They just live what they live what they live driven by what is in their own mind. They never take the time to realize that what is in their mind is not necessarily what is in the mind of that someone else.

This is very evident when life activities lead to arguments. Why do people argue? Because they do not like what another person is saying or doing. That other person is saying or doing something—they said or did something that you do not like. Thus, confrontation is given birth to.

In an actual argument, the two sides of the story are verbally presented. One person is saying or yelling out their point of view while the other person is doing the same with their. With this, the two differing points of view and the motivation(s), leading to the action(s), that lead to the argument, can be heard. Life isn't always like this, however. Some times/many times people keep their point of view locked into their own mind. Then, why they did what they did can never truly be known. This does not mean that they did not do what they did for some self-motivate, foolish, or possibly even not-thinking reason. Yet, it is kept to themselves; lost to the knowing of all others forever.

So, what does this leave us with? Answer: There is what you think, there is what motivates you to say and do what you do, but there is also what that someone else thinks, there is also what motivates them to say and do what they do. If you don't take this into consideration all you are is lost in your own mind game. All you are is a selfish individual saying, doing, and being driven to reactions based upon nothing more than what is defined by your own mind.

In life, everybody has a reason. That does not necessarily make their reason right or just; but it is nonetheless their reason. You have yours, they have theirs. Only the desired ultimate outcome, which is defined by each individual individually, can ever be the deciding factor for who was ultimately right and who was universally wrong.

You need to always remember there are other factors at play, in all life interactions, other than simply your own. And, no matter how you want any life situation to culminating, it is only you that is laying down that definition. But remember there are always at least two minds at play in everything life involved. Maybe you desire the same outcome as that someone else, maybe you don't. But, no matter what you are thinking, you can be assured that any person living any life event with you is assuredly thinking something else. Remember this. It may make you a more understating individual.

The Reality of the Reality
17/Oct/2021 08:05 AM

I often speak and write about each of us living the reality of our reality. ...Being as absolutely truthful as possible in order for us to be our best/truest self in order personally grow in a positive manner and to help the all of humanity in the best way that we can.

This being said, I was flipping through the music video channels last night, before I went to bed, as I often tend to do. I watched this music video, *"Hard Feelings,"* by what I thought was a female singer, *Miquela.* My lady asked a question about her that I could not answer so I grabbed my phone to look up more information about her. As it turns out, she is not a she at all. She is a *"Fictional Character,"* a *"Digital Avatar,"* a *"Virtual CGI Influencer."* This really surprised me as she appeared to be so real in the video. Anyway... She is not real. She is not a real person. She is not a real singer. She is a computer construct.

Now, I don't know how they do that. She looked so real. I'm sure some of you people out there know way more about all of that than I. There is apparently not even a person behind the scenes signing the song; like say in *The Archies* or *Milli Vanilli.* The singing is all also constructed. ...Don't know how they do it but it sounds pretty good.

In checking a bit deeper, her creators even gave her a gap between her front teeth and some freckles to show that she has imperfections to make her more appealing ??? Okay, I used to have a gap between my two front teeth.

Somehow/somewhere along the line of my life it closed by itself, however. I guess my teeth shifted. I guess that makes me less appealing. ☺

As far as Miquela goes, think how many young boys and men hold her in the realms of fantasy and possibility in their minds. I know when I was young I had hopes to meet girls like that. I remember I had a fantasy about Laurie Partridge, (Susan Dey), of the TV show, the *Partridge Family.* I mean, she was only a couple of years older than me and as I lived in L.A. where it was not/is not uncommon to see celebrities all the time, I thought/hoped I may bump into her. Awh, the foolish dreams of a child... Anyway, but all the people pumping fantasy towards *Miquela;* where do those fantasies go?

Life always changes. The reality of the reality of life always changes. Now, it changes fairly rapidly. This is particularly true since we entered first the computer age and later the digital age where all things can be fabricated, even people.

So, here we are. The reality is no longer the reality. It all has become *maya,* illusion. We are now presented with the falsity of reality all of the time. What can/what should we do?

All we can do is hold tightly to our own truth. We need to keep the REAL as real as possible. For now there is all of these artificial constructs out there. And yes, I'm sure there will be more.

There will always be the lies that are told that are presented as the truth. But, the truth is the truth is the truth. Sometimes, you just have to dig deep to find it out.

So be true to you. Be true to others. Tell yourself the truth. Tell others the truth. Let them know what is real to you and keep your reality as real as possible. For there are a lot of illusions out there that will try to suck you into their realms of fantasy. But remember, a fantasy is only that; a fantasy. A lie is only a lie no matter how pretty it is packaged. But, the truth, what is real in this here and this now, can never be altered. As long as you live in the reality of the reality, your reality will be true and you can be/become the best you that you can be. And yes, abiding in the truth of reality, you may even be able to help someone else along on their path.

Providing fantasy is never the pathway to reality. Truly embracing your reality is the only way of fundamentally experiencing and living the truth.

* * *

16/Oct/2021 05:57 PM

Until you realize and admit that it is all your fault there is no chance for self-actualization or self-realization.

All Life is Suffering

15/Oct/2021 09:57 AM

In certain Theravada Buddhist sects it is taught that, *"All Life is suffering."* If you look to the Pali Canons you will see that, *"Duḥkha," "Suffering,"* is one of primary elements in understanding life. ...That as long as you possess any desires, as we all do, your life will be bound by a lack of fulfillment, equaling suffering.

If you look to your life, take a moment and define a time or the times when you felt you were really suffering. If you look to these moments, most likely you will find that the reason your felt so bad was that you were not getting what you wanted: whether this was the love you wanted, the possession you wanted, the position you wanted, or the respect you felt you deserved. Or that someone or something was or is doing something to you or did something to you that you do/did not like. This tells us that it is very easy to understand the cause of our suffering. But, how few are the people who are willing to consciously realize this truth.

You want, you desire, you don't get, you suffer.

In life, we are all bound by death. Death is one of the most painful experiences there is. There is the pain in losing someone you love. There is also the ultimate pain of you dying. Thus, you are no more. But, though this is a central reality to living, how few are the people who ever allow themselves to face this fact and accept the consequences of this living reality? All things are going to die.

Though the truth of the cause of suffering is very evident, all people seem to hope to chart a path away from it. Some live in denial. Some take drugs. And, there are many forms of drugs other than simple intoxicants. There are people who fall into love over and over again. There are people who fall into lust over and over again. There are people lost into the stimulation of their job. There are the thrill seekers. There are people seeking to buy that whatever and then when they have that whatever they must have something more. There are some who embrace a constant sense of anger, looking for trouble. And, the list goes on and on. But, no matter how one seeks to avoid the fact of the fact, in each person's life suffering is an inevitable reality.

But, here's the catch, you do not have to allow suffering to control you. You can take control of it. Now, I get it, this is very easy for someone to say when they are not the one embroiled in the sense of suffering. But, for most of us, we do not have to look too deeply into our lives to remember when we were suffering. The difference is, how one/how you defines, prepares for, and embraces that suffering.

The fact is, when you hurt you hurt. That's the end of the story. That is you suffering. But, can you take control of your consciousness, of your thought patterns, and find a new way of encountering that unfortunate reality? Thus, finding meaning instead of only pain.

Where all this begins is in how you encounter your life. For example, when you are living your day-to-day life how much time do you spent feeling the okay-ness of it all. When you are laying in bed, do you ever take the time to think, *"Wow, this feels okay. I am warm, I am comfortable, life is not too bad."* When you are driving down the street and a good song comes on the radio do you ever just sit back into the perfection of the moment and truly enjoy that music driven experience and allow yourself to consciously feel the subtle goodness of that moment?

You see, this is where people begin to set the stage of their life and how they will encounter and define the not so good times. You must take the time to realize, embellish, and consciously encounter it when that good is happening. In fact, you must train your mind to allow yourself to feel the goodness as simple as that goodness may be.

Think about how many times you were living some moment, (that felt pretty good), and you didn't even take notice of it until that experience was over? It was only then that you realized that what you had lived was really nice. Think about if you had been fully in that moment—if you have been consciously aware, think how much more you could have truly lived, truly experienced in that time in your life.

You really need to train your mind to appreciate your moment.

All life is defined by time. It is define by the time that we have to be what we are and live what we live. The problem in most people lives is, they do not take notice of the moment(s) of okay. Then, when they are hit with the sucker punch of the not okay they have no goodness to fall back on. Thus, they become wholly lost in their suffering.

So yes, there is suffering in life. There's no way around it. But, it is your developed array of the memories of goodness that can hold you through those times of hurt. You can allow the suffering to define your life or you can have developed enough memories of goodness that they will guide you through even the most painful of times.

Realize there is suffering in life. And yes, you will feel it someday. But, embrace—bring in all the goodness that you can as you pass through your days—then, at least, you will know that there is also grand goddess and feel-goodness in this world/in your life.

*   *   *

15/Oct/2021 07:25 AM

What happens when you've done something good but no one knows you did it?

*   *   *

14/Oct/2021 11:29 AM

How bad do you feel when something bad happens to someone who did something bad to you?

Do Your Research

13/Oct/2021 09:40 AM

It's kind of funny... I got this email this morning from a guy pitching a script to me. Of course, the guy states, that it has a great plot and could be made into sequel after sequel. Okay...

Hello. I'm a Zen Filmmaker!!! Do your research!!! I don't use scripts!!! And, do I look like the kind of guy that could finance your project? I shoot my movies for like $300.00. Now, if you want to talk about financing one of my films, that's another story. ☺

You know, I always find it funny—this whole film game thing... There are all these people, writing all these scripts, trying to get them financed and produced. And yes, some of them are brought up. But, for anyone who is actually in the middle of the film game and you go to an agency that handles screenwriters, it is scary the stacks upon stacks upon stacks upon stacks of scripts that are out there—screenplays that will never get made.

I wonder if there is a heaven for dead screenplays?

You know, it's not that the screenplays are necessary bad. It's that they will never make their way into the right hands that could/can do something with them. I mean, think how many bad movies you've seen where you're just shaking your head about the poor or unrealistic story development and/or the ridiculous dialogue. That movie got written, got financed, and got made.

Hell, back in the day, I used to write scripts. ...Until I realized that art can never be memorized, it can only be lived.

You know, every now and then, over these past many-many years of being in the film game, someone hits me up to finance the making of their film. I guess that's okay... Thanks for thinking about me. But, to take this to a deeper level of life, what is actually going on here? Is it someone thinking about someone else? Is it someone trying to help someone else? Or, is someone trying to help themselves? I think the answer is obvious.

...Promising how much money a movie based on a screenplay you wrote could make is ego-fueled speculation at best. Every screenwriter thinks their script is the best script ever written. Find flaws in it, tell them it's not that good; that it's just rehashing the same story that's been told a thousand times before and look out! They will call you a liar and hate you.

You know, when people have come to me offering me roles in films, music videos, commercials, and stuff like that, I appreciate it. They are reaching out to me and at least trying to offer me something. But, most of Hollywood is not like that. They are all about their ME.

Don Jackson used to go into this rant as everyone used to come at him trying to get him to give them money to get their movie made. He would scream, *"Me, me, me, me, me, me!"* I think I actually put one of those rants into one of the docs I made about him. ...He used to love to have himself filmed all the time so after he passed I was left with a lot of very useable footage. Anyway...

What it all boils down to is people want something from someone else. They want them to finance their dream. And, I get it, Hollywood is an ego drive game. But, the moment any of that happens, art is gone. Then it becomes nothing more than someone trying to getting something for themselves.

So, people... Here's the paradox... The Zen Koan, if you will... *"What happens when you pitch a screenplay to a filmmaker that doesn't use screenplays?"* The answer is...

Cog in the Wheel

13/Oct/2021 08:46 AM

Cog in the wheel… I always thought that was a weird expression. I mean, what does it actually mean? Sure, we all kinda know what it is supposed to mean; someone who is a supportive element to the overall movement of a whatever… But, that term… I don't know? Just weird…

It's not used very much anymore. So, I guess, like so many things life, it will eventually fade away. But, all this being said, when it comes to you/to me, what does it really mean? How do you function in relation to the overall whole?

I think most people don't really think about this. For most it is more about doing their job, whatever that job may be. Some love their job. Many hate their job. Others are somewhere in between. But, for pretty much everyone (me included) they have hopes and dreams of that greater whatever.

Some act to achieve those dreams. I know I do. I try. Others just hold them in their head. But, the reality of the reality of the reality is, we are all held captive by our circumstance; be that mental, physical, or whatever… And though we can try, and some will achieve, we are all, nonetheless, left to being nothing more than a cog in the wheel.

For me, I have watched this process very closely as I have passed through my life. I've met a lot of people who wanted that grand something, but for that whatever reason they could never achieve it; which has left some very bitter. For example, I watched this one old guy for maybe thirty years now. Once upon a time he was a nice, kind, very giving person. I truly thought he had lived a good life. As his life progressed and what he had envisioned for his life never came to materialize, he became this massive liar, telling these grand tales about worldwide espionage; giant tales like you read in a spy novel or see in a film. He was/is not happy having simply been a cog in the wheel. He desired more and when more never materialized he made up his more in his head and he now tells his stories to anyone who will listen.

As someone who has spent a good portion of my life in the film game, I have watched the process of desire verses reality a lot. Like one of the first things I always pose to my students whenever I teach a class, *"What is the number one rule of filmmaking?"* Answer, *"Everybody lies."* ...They all have grand tales of what they've done, who they've done it with, and where they will end up.

I think back to this one dinner I had with a filmmaking friend, my lady, and this guy I had put in a few films as an actor. When we sat down it was like this unbelievable pouring out of bullshit from this guy's mouth. I mean, it was scary! Dropping names. Saying what he was going to do, who he was going to do it with, and what grand reality was coming his direction. My friend and I played it cool. My lady, on the other, the minute this guy got up to go to the bathroom, she loudly exclaims, *"What a bunch of bullshit!"* I know he heard her statement as he was just a couple of feet away. I gave her the, shuuuu. But, the guy came back for more.

This all raises the question, if you project a false reality does it make it true? Of course not. But, for someone who may believe you, then they believe you. Thus, in their mind what you have said is true. So???

Again, everybody, well at least most, want to be that grand something. As a filmmaker I have watched and witnessed how important every member of the filmmaking team is on the set. Especially on the larger production films. Everybody has a purpose. And yes, some of the jobs may be less glorious than others—some may be easier than others, but they are all necessary. All of the people that are there are all a cog in the wheel.

Like on the lower budget sets, like my films… You always need to have a Capitan of the Ship. But, your production can either sail or sink by how strong your 1st Mate is. I've worked with some people who were a great benefit to the production. I've also worked with people who are just the opposite. Me, I've been in both positions. When I was the 1st Mate, I put my ego in check, and I did my upmost to make the production as good as it could be. Not everyone is like that, however. Ego and desire play a big part in all things life, especially when they are attached to a person who is in a position of power—however large or small that power may be. But, ego and desire do not get the job done. Doing the job gets the job done. And, if you don't do it, nothing gets done.

So, what does this tell us? Where does this leave us? It tells us that we are all cogs in the wheel, no matter where we find ourselves in life.

We must focus on what we can do—what we can get done and then do it. Ego, desire, and even lying are projected all the time but what do they equal? Not very much. But, if you can find yourself where you are, do what you can do, you can live a proud, good life understanding that you move this ALL reality forward by being the best you, you can be and by doing the best job you can do defined by wherever you find yourself in life.

We all have desires and fantasies to be great and grand. But, you cannot let those things keep you from doing what you actually can do.

Do what you can do. Be what you can be. If you're just a cog in the wheel; great! At least at the end of your days you'll know you contributed—you did something as opposed to nothing.

* * *

13/Oct/2021 08:45 AM

The years of your life will pass away. What are you going to do to with them to make your time have meant something?

* * *

13/Oct/2021 08:44 AM

Sometimes you just have to live with the choices you've made.

The Spiritual Mask

12/Oct/2021 12:59 PM

Pretty much the moment anyone claims to be a spiritual anything that pretty much means they are not.

Throughout my years of walking on this spiritual path, I have met many a person who proclaimed a Spiritual Something. And yes, some of them were very famous and a couple did appear to have various forms of *Siddha, "Spiritual Powers."* Most, however, were/are simply self-proclaimed nothings, that just defined themselves as, *"Spiritual."* But, all a person like that does is to leave a wake of broken people who once believed but were taken advantage of.

I think back to when I taught my very first class on yoga that was not done at an ashram. It was via the *California State University, Northridge Experimental College.* If you feel like it, you can see the ad for that class on the Sundries page of this website. Me, I was like twenty years old.

My class was on the various aspects of yoga; meaning the various branches and how one could practice and use the various techniques. There was another person teaching a class on Kundalini Yoga at the same time. He was just your average white guy who had taken Sikh initiation via Yogi Bahjan. There were a lot of Caucasian Sikhs around at that time: wearing their turbans and growing their beards.

Anyway, this guy required that all of his students bring him flowers before each class. When two of my students asked me if they needed to bring me flowers, I just smiled and said, *"No."*

My thought was, however, *"Who is this guy, self-believing that he is in a position to deserve flowers simply because he is teaching something that he learned from someone else?"* Anyway... That's just one example.

Certainly, I spent a lot of time with Swami Satchidanada. A lot of time with him and a lot more time with his other disciples. He was always great to me. I think he was amused at how young I was when I joined the ranks. But, in his later years, he had his detractors. Women who claimed he did what he did with them. This, when he was claiming to be celibate and telling all of us, his disciples, to do the same. I've written about this subject in several places in the past and what I think about it. But, more importantly, I have also long stated that if a teacher can't be more than his or her students, then what does that leave the students with?

A teacher should be more than their students. A teacher should set the ideal example. This fact, has caused me to turn away from several teachers throughout my lifetime.

Were they fakes? This is for the individual to judge. But, if you don't lead by example, then what are you actually teaching?

I won't go into some of the very hardcore fakes I've encountered. As I have written about them in the past. But remember, simply because someone claims to be a *Spiritual Something* that does not mean that is what they truly are.

If you look to people like Tenzin Gyatso, the fourteenth Dalai Lama, there is an example of a person who lives what he teaches. Though Tibetan tradition places him in an exalted position, he never relishes in that. He is just a cordial, joking man who simply lives the life that karma gave him. J. Krishnamurti was very much the same. The Buddha himself when asked if he was teacher he said, *"I'm just a man."* But, how few are the teachers that do not relish in their position—that do not take advantage and attempted to live an embellished lifestyle due to them being what they claim to be? And, this goes on throughout all teachings and religions; throughout time.

What am I saying here? If you are drawn to the spiritual path you really need to become hyper aware and keep your eyes open. There are a lot of people who are claiming what they claim that are only driven by self-defined ego. Do you really want to learn from a teacher like that?

Mind Watching

12/Oct/2021 07:21 AM

Throughout the centuries meditation techniques have been developed in order to calm the mind of the individual and cause them to enter into a refined state of consciousness where they may encounter a deeper wisdom and possibly even god-consciousness. The thing is, very few people ever practice any of these techniques of meditation. How about you? Some people may poke at them for a moment at the end of a yoga or martial art class, a few may even sit down and try to meditate for a moment here or there but very-very few ever take meditation on as a life course where they actually follow the path of meditation allowing it to reveal the indescribable things that can only be known when they are known.

This is not bad or good. This is just the way it is. Though pretty much everyone known about meditation, very few people try its practice.

This being said, there is a technique that does not take a lifetime of practice for it to be revealing of the True Individual Self. I refer to this technique as Mind Watching. It's very easy.

Here we go...

You can do this now but it is better to perform when you are in a mentally passive state of mind; perhaps when you are going to sleep, maybe when you have just woken up, or maybe when you have relaxed as you are sitting by a stream or the ocean or wherever. It's best done when you are in a clam state of mind.

Close your eyes. Feel the calmness in your being. Allow your mind to be silent. Don't try to force this like people do in meditation. Simply allow your thoughts to be your thoughts with no forced definition.

Now, take your consciousness to that place where you can look at your mind—that place where you can watch your thoughts. There is that place in all of us, where we can see and view ourselves. Some people call this, The Witness.

To do this technique you simply need to remain in that state of observational calmness for a moment or a long as you feel comfortable doing it.

Look deeply into you. See who you really are. You can do this by following your thoughts. Why are you thinking what you are thinking? Why do you think what you think? Or, you can simply allowing this witnessing mind to look deep into the core of your inner being. Who are you? What are you? Why are you?

There is no right or wrong way to do this technique. Just as there is no right or wrong answer(s) you will find. All there is, is you. Allow this technique to reveal who and what you truly are.

The only thing you want to be careful of is not allowing your ego to drive you. You don't want that grand or false thing that you believe you are to be the captain of your ship for all that will lead you to is folly. In other words, be humble and truthful in your mental quest.

Assuredly, your focused mind will be called away by your random racing thoughts relatively quickly. You can call your mind back to the focus of this technique as many times as you wish or your can simply allow your thoughts to drag you away. Your choice. But, this is a very simply technique that has the potential to reveal all kinds of stuff about you. You can practice it once or your can do it whenever you feel like.

Give is a try. You never know what you may find out about yourself.

*   *   *

11/Oct/2021 03:46 PM

Is your life defined by what you have done or what someone else has done to you?

* * *

11/Oct/2021 11:25 AM

You can't tell someone to care about their karma when they don't care about their karma.

They will only realize the implications of their actions when they are slapped across the face with them.

Death Should Not Be a Game

11/Oct/2021 07:32 AM

I was waiting for the new episode of *The Walking Dead* to come on last night so I was flipping channels. I came upon the premiere of this new show following the police of Louisiana that handle the wild life patrol.

First of all, let me state, I used to really enjoy shows like COPS and Live PD. In fact, COPS was one of my biggest influences when I entered the filmmaking game. I loved that style of raw cinematography and reality. But, then came this age of... I don't even know what to call it. I guess, *"Political Correctness."* And, they took shows like Live PD and COPS off the air. Once upon a time you could pretty much find an episode of COPS playing somewhere on some channel day or night. Now, nada. What has remained is a couple of shows that feature Game Wardens and the like. Not nearly as intense but... It is a minor fix if you want a dose of reality policing TV.

So, I'm watching that show and this one female officer was lamenting about how they may have to take this six year old boys first kill of a deer away form him. She was sad as she had killed her first deer when she was six. Then, the show went to another officer talking to another father who was so proud of his young son's kill of a deer. Wow...

Now, I get it, I'm a city kid and you people from rural America and other places grow up with a different set of standards than I did. But, when I see a deer, I just think how pure and beautiful it is. I love to watch it move and live its life. I never think about killing it. I mean, isn't it understood that people that grow up to be psycho killers begin by killing animals when they are young. Now, I'm not saying that about these kids, but it seems like they are being skilled to kill. Then, when they do kill, their actions are applauded. I don't know... I just don't see that as right.

I have never gone hunting. I never would. They only experience I ever had with hunting was when I was about twelve or thirteen and my mother, who was originally from the mid-west, and I visited her hometown this one time. My distant cousin, via marriage, was going hunting. He invited me. I didn't want to go. I was all into Eastern spirituality and such. But, my mother insisted. We're out there in the woods and this guy goes nuts. He goes on a rampage killing every raccoon he could find. It was horrible! I write a longer, more in-depth, piece about this experience in my book, *Zen: Tales for the Journey,* if you're interested. Everything about that experience was repulsive. It was truly traumatizing.

Why does anyone want to kill poor wild animals like deers and raccoons or any other helpless animal that has no chance against a gun? Everything about that process just seems wrong!

I guess it all come down to the question, what reality are you living? What reality were you taught to live? What reality do you teach your children to live? And, how does that reality shape the mind of society? How does it shape the all and the everything? Should killing ever be a game? And, where is your TRUTH if you kill for sport?

I'm sorry, killing on any level is just not right. And, if you kill for sport, if you use a gun against a helpless animals, what does that make you? A sportsman? I don't think so. I believe the definition of you and your actions should be much more critical.

Think before you ever consider the killing of anything. And, I mean anything. Death is death and once something is dead it is never coming back. The killing of any life should never be something that you take pride in.

*   *   *

10/Oct/2021 01:37 PM

What do you do when you find out you were wrong?

Try This
10/Oct/2021 06:55 AM

Try This:

Do something nice for someone you don't really like today.

Don't make a big deal about it, don't tell them about it, don't think you're going to get some good karma for doing it; just do it.

Watch how the world becomes just a little bit better.

Try This:

Do something nice for someone you do really like today.

Don't make a big deal about it, don't tell them about it, don't think you're going to get some good karma for doing it; just do it.

Watch how the world becomes just a little bit better.

Every time you do something nice for someone everything becomes just a little bit better.

*   *   *

09/Oct/2021 12:03 PM

Why does everyone need something to worship?

*   *   *

09/Oct/2021 12:02 PM

What can you do today that will make your tomorrow better?

What can you do today that will make someone else's tomorrow better?

What can you do today that will make everybody's tomorrow better?

No Ultimate Outcome
09/Oct/2021 07:29 AM

I know people who have lived a very spiritual lifestyle for over the past fifty years. They entered the Eastern tradition of spirituality and never left. In some cases these people follow the monastic path and they are still living it today. Some have taught the various aspects of yoga and meditation for all of these years. Most refrained from the pursuit of ego and simply lived a very humble existence. Though I am sure they made their friends along the way and they may have helped some people, how did what they offered, what they lived, change anything? Though they lived a tried and true life, there was no ultimate outcome to all that they did.

Like I have long believed, and have stated many times in many places, the most contributive martial artists I have known were those teachers who ran a small school, did not care about rank or prestige, never claimed, *"My Kung Fu is better than your Kung Fu,"* and simply taught their students their understandings of these ancient systems of self-defense. What they taught their students is something that will stay with that person throughout a lifetime. This is why I always suggest, to the all and the everyone, that they study the martial arts, at least for a time, because it truly will give you something that will accompany you throughout your life.

With that example, we have someone who does have an ultimate outcome. With the previous example, we find someone who is seemingly walking an ideal path in life but not actually contributing a lot to the overall evolution of anyone or anything. What does this tell us? Do you ever contemplate how what one person does or does not do will affect the all and the everything?

Perhaps the better question is, what will what you are doing with your life ultimately equal? What will be the ultimate outcome of your life contribution?

Most people fall into a pattern of doing. They live through their childhood, they go to school, then they get a job. Maybe they get married. Maybe they have a family. They live through the various trials and the tribulations that we all encounter. But, at the end of their days what was their ultimate outcome?

Most people do not seem to posses the desire or the focus to look at the bigger picture as they pass through their life. They only live their moment. And, though living in the moment has been taught to be a supreme state of consciousness; is it? Or, is it simply an excuse—a way to make your time pass without looking too deeply into what is actually going on with your life?

So, ask yourself this question, what will be the ultimate outcome of your life if you stay on the path that you are walking? There's no right or wrong answer, there is just you being/becoming honest with yourself.

Take the time to truly ponder this question. It may cause you to take a long hard look at your existence and possibly change your pathway, if necessary.

*   *   *

08/Oct/2021 04:00 PM

How many bits of supposed ancient wisdom has someone quoted, that you believed, but those words were never spoken by a venerable sage?

How many things have you been told happen that did not actually happen but you believed what you were told to be true?

How many things did someone claim they saw but they never saw yet you believed what they claimed to have witnessed?

How many things have you believed that simply were not true?

The Choices That You Choose

08/Oct/2021 07:39 AM

Your life is defined by the choices that you make. Each next step that you encounter in your life is predicated upon that last choice that you made.

Some believe that their life was set on a course of events based upon where they grew up, how they grew up, and what they did or did not have when they were growing up. Others believe that their choices are not their own. They are forced to make their choices by the predicaments they are given due to the actions of someone else. As true as those two ideas may be, the ultimate definition of your life comes down to the choices that you make in each life situation no matter where, how, or by whom you arrived at the need to make that choice.

We are all defined by the choices we are allowed to make. What gives us our next set of life choices? The choices we previously made defines where we find ourselves in this here and this now.

Some of the choices you make are very memorable. You made that choice and it changed the entire direction of your life. Other choices you make are so small that they are forgotten pretty much the moment you made them. They were made, you did what you did, lived what you lived, and then you moved on to make your next choice. No matter the size or the scale of that choice you made, it is that choice that defines your next choice, which then defines your next choice after that and so on. We are all defined by the last choice that we made.

How much time do you spend contemplating the choices that you make? Are you one of those people that just goes for it—never really thinks too deeply about the impact of your choices and then either basks in the rewards or suffers the consequences? Or, are you someone who thinks out with precision every choice you make—you ponder the ramifications of every choice before that choice is made?

How often do you regret the choices that you have made? How often do you feel bad about a choice you made that negativity affected the life of someone else? How often do you lie to try to redefine the choices that you have made? If this is the case with any of your choices, do you ever truly ask yourself what caused you to make that choice in the first place?

Just as other peoples choices have an impact on you and the next set of choices you will be presented with, your choices can and will affect the next set of choices another person or persons will be presented with. How much time do you spend contemplating how your choices are going to affect that someone else? Do you contemplate this and/or question it at all? Or, are all your choices simply defined by the selfishness of your own mind?

A choice is the defining factor of all of our lives. Shouldn't this be one of the most hallowed elements of life that each person undertakes? But, is it? How deeply do you contemplate your choices? Do you truly question how that next choice you will make is going to affect your life, the life of anyone else involved, and how it will create your next choice?

Choice is the defining factor of your life. It is the one thing that no on else can truly control because it is you who ultimately decides what choice you will make. What choice are you going to make next? Your life, your choice?

*   *   *

07/Oct/2021 02:58 PM

How long can you sit in silence?

* * *

07/Oct/2021 10:09 AM

Who is going to love you after you die?

The Many Levels of Consciousness

07/Oct/2021 08:05 AM

In Sanskrit, there are many words that describe the understanding of Consciousness. Perhaps the most universally used word is, *"Chit,"* but many other words are employed to define the various levels of consciousness, such as, *"Saṃjñāna," "Saṃjñananā," "Caitanya,"* and, *"Bodha."* In fact, there are many more. In English, however, we are left with only one primary word describing, *"Consciousness."* It is a blanket term devised to be individually interrupted.

The more clear, highly defined definition in Sanskrit is perhaps a better way of understanding the many levels of consciousness. But, as Sanskrit is a dying language, and so few speak it, what we are left with is what we are left with.

Take a moment right now. Ask yourself, *"How do you define consciousness?" "What does consciousness mean to you?"* Is it simply your state of being; you are alive? Or, is it something more profound; you progressing and transcending into a higher realm of Self Awareness?

Continue this thought process for a moment more and ponder, *"How much time do you spend in rising your consciousness each day?"* Is it a just a passing thought, whenever that thought passes, is it a moment, a minute, an hour, or not at all?

Most people don't think too much about consciousness; particularly raising their consciousness. They are too busy thinking about all of their Life Stuff. But, what does it mean to ponder higher consciousness? What does it mean to you? And, if you do ever think about it, what do you do to make yourself a more conscious individual?

Take a few moments and think about it. You may come up with some interesting realizations.

Accused of Telling a Lie
AKA Roll with the Punches

06/Oct/2021 02:51 PM

It's kind of funny… Well, funny in that very sad sort of way…

Anyway, I got this four page handwritten letter today. Wow, I have not received a handwritten letter in I can't tell you when… But, it's been decades.

Wait! Thinking about it… The last handwritten letter I received was from Dr. Wayne Dyer in the early 1990s. It was a FU letter that really showed his true nature. Not the calm spiritual guy that he portrayed to the world. I used to have an essay with a copy of our correspondence and that letter up on this website. But, when he passed away I took it down. Don't speak ill of the dead and all that…

Anyway, the letter I got today was from that guy who hit and totaled my car a few weeks ago.

To refresh all you Blog Reader's memories… A guy went jamming down the wrong side of the street in his junky old Ford pickup to get to the open median area of the street due to a traffic jam and he sideswiped my car killing it. Sad, I really liked that car. Still haven't got another car yet. Apparently, due to the pandemic the new car dealerships have no inventory and the used car prices are sky high. So??? Though he jammed off from the scene of the crime he did return about fifteen minutes later. He probably thought I snapped a photo of his license plate or something, which I did. The guy didn't have insurance.

Anyway, I guess my insurance company contacted him and when they were talking to him he threatened to sue me. And now, today, I get this handwritten letter, obviously written for the eyes of the reader, claiming it was all my fault; completely turning the truth about what happened into some projected fantasy. Like most people who damage or hurt the life of someone else he never apologized for his actions or tried to make anything right. He even wrote, either I or my insurance company representative is lying. Of course, he says if he doesn't hear from me he's going to take me to court. Okay… I've got photos, dude! That's my proof of whose at fault. And, all you had to have was insurance and none of this nonsense would be going on.

You know, I learned a long time ago, when I first got into the film industry, that you never threaten to sue someone. You either sue them or you don't. I also learned that you really have to want to sue someone because it costs a lot of money. Money you may never get back because what do people do when they lose a big lawsuit? They go bankrupt. Equaling no money, no matter who wins. And, if you do sue someone they are most certainly going to sue you back. So, threatening to sue someone is just stupid.

I think back to early '92 when a guy hit me from behind when I was on my Harley. It killed my Harley. Again, the guy had no insurance. I was really going through a lot at that moment of my life. I had just gotten majorly fucked over, financially and otherwise, by the Executive Producer of *The Roller Blade Seven* and my Porsche had blown its transmission. So, I just didn't need that to happen. The difference with him and the guy who hit me with his truck was that the guy who hit my Harley had a sister who was a lawyer. In-house counsel and all that. He got away with it. I was left with my fully customized Harley in a dead heap. The guy who customized it gave me $2,000.00 for the remaining parts. That's it! Again, the driver lied about what happened but he had a sister lawyer willing to say or do whatever it took to win for the sake of her brother.

Like I have discussed in the past, a liar always lies. And, they will lie and deny, until their dying day, that they are a liar. Then, they are the first one to turn it all around and call someone else a liar even when that other person is telling the truth. Have you ever met anyone like that? Lairs are a bad breed.

We all make mistakes or have accidents in life. Sure, they suck. But, you really need to own it. Not lie about it. Because if you lie, all that makes you is a liar. And, no one wants to be known as a liar.

You know, it seems like the shit always hits the fan when you just don't need it. I mean, I'm dealing with the loss of my cat a couple of days ago. Just really sad. That guy killed my car a couple of weeks ago. Now, I've got to figure out where I can get another car and maybe another Persian cat, as my other cat is now all bummed out and lonely—he lived with her his entire life. Anyone know any breeders?

Anyway, I just don't need it! I don't need to get a handwritten letter from that guy trying to turn the story around. I don't need any of it!

It reminds me of this other time, way back in the way back when... I had brought this guy into the film game. He had taken a few of my classes and he seemed like a nice guy who really wanted to get his feet wet in the industry. I was happy to help. I never really understood why he got pissed at me, but I guess I had made a joke or something that put him off??? (I tend to be a bit of a joker). Anyway, my father-in-law, who I was very close to, (my last drinkin' buddy), was on his way out. He asked his daughter and I to come down to the OC, where he lived, and help him get to the hospitable. As I was driving my pager started blowing up. I was getting voice mail after voice mail from that guy just going off on me. He had my mobile number but he didn't want to call it. Why, I don't know? When I called him, he hung up on me. I guess he didn't want to discuss and/or hear my side of the goings-on... Then, he started calling all the cast of the film we were shooting, telling them what a fucked up human being I was. (What kind of person does something like that?) Thus, they all started calling me on my voice mail, wondering what was up. Wow... It was just crazy. If you have something to say, say it directly to the person. All this while I was trying to focus on the last hours of my father-in-laws life.

It always seems that's how life goes... When it comes at you, it comes at you.

But, here's the facts... When it does come at you, who cares? Only you. It's you, it's not them. Think about all the pain that is going on all over the world right now. Think about all of the major catastrophes and the small things where just one individual is involved. Think about the last time you were in pain. Who was there for you? Who stopped the attackers? Who took your pain away? Who helped you? Where's the god equation in any of this?

And, all liars do is try to blame the someone else.

It comes down to not only how you deal with a situation but also how any other person involved deals with that situation. It comes down to who is willing to step from the shadows and help you.

Me, I always try to be as upfront and honest as I can. Yeah, I have my perspective but I always try to understand the other person's perspective. When that guy finally came back to the scene of the crime, he seemed like a nice enough guy. I was very cordial to him. I didn't go off on him at all. I was nice even though my car sat there in the middle of the street completely unmovable—never to drive again.

Maybe I was wrong. Me being wrong about people is not uncommon. My problem is, I care. But, I don't have a sister who is a lawyer and no lawyer is revealing themselves from the grand abyss to protect me from anything—not even handwritten letters. So, I guess I just have to deal with it all myself.

Probably most of us have been in a position like this, once upon a time or two in our life; have you? Not fun. In fact, it's just stupid. But, this is life. Not everyone is nice and honest; true and god fearing. Most are just in it for themselves. How about you? How much do you care about anyone but you? And, if you do care, what do you do about that caring? Who do you help: why and when?

How Much Do You Think About What I Think About?

06/Oct/2021 09:32 AM

In life, we are each damned to the condition of being locked into our own mind. Meaning, we are who we are. We think what we think. Though time, life, study, and experiences we each become a unique personification of what we could or should become but are we ever allowed to move free from our own mind?

Some people, particularly when they are in love, truly think about that other person. They listen to what they have to say. They try to embody their suggestions. And, they do all they can to make that other person's life better. But, how few are the people who behave like this? How few are the people that ever step outside of themselves—outside of their own mind to actually focus their thoughts on that someone else? Mostly, all life is defined by a person who is locked into their own mind and only thinking what they think and doing for themselves.

For each of us, we listen and we learn from the people we choose to listen to and learn from. Okay... But, how does that change anything for anyone except the person doing the listening and the learning?

Most people are very willing to take. They are willing to take the knowledge someone else speaks, as long as they like what they have to say. They are willing to receive any gifts that are offered but what are they willing to give? Most people never think about any of this. Why? Because they are so lost in their own mind that they never take the time to step outside of that mind. They never take the time to question what they can give back. What this leaves us with is the world as the world is. ...A world lost in the individual mind.

Throughout the East and even in some Western philosophic traditions it is spoken about that, *"We are all one."* But, are we? No. We are all our individual mind. Yes, some people care more about others than someone else. Yes, some people take other people's feelings and thoughts more into consideration than do others. But, that is just them doing what their mind wants them to do.

So, what does this leave us with? It leaves us with you. What do you think about? Who do you think about? What do you do for those people and things that you think about? Or, is all that you do focused upon you?

I say it all time, this is world is created by you. You could make it a better place. You could help and do positive things for the people and things that you think about. But, will you?

*   *   *

05/Oct/2021 10:10 AM

If you don't care more about the people, you've hurt than the people you've helped your thoughts are focused in the wrong direction.

*   *   *

05/Oct/2021 10:10 AM

If you never personally read a book how can you know what actually was written?

You Should've

05/Oct/2021 07:18 AM

For each of us in life there are those things that we get the idea to do. In some cases we only think and dream of that doing. In other cases we actually look into it. But, for whatever reason, we never follow through. Then, maybe a day, a week, a month, a year, or many years later we really realize that we should have done that thing as it would have made our life so much better—it would have made us that so much more.

There are many reasons that we do not do that do. Maybe it's money. We didn't have enough. Money, or the lack thereof, always seems to be one of the biggest deterrents in life. Maybe it was that we didn't have the focus. Maybe it was that someone talked us out of doing it. Maybe it is we just got sacred or we came to believe that we couldn't do it. Whatever the case, we are left with the definition of our life defined by that thing we didn't do.

As this COVID-19 pandemic came upon us and most of us found ourselves in lock down, many people set about learning that something new. But, how many of those people followed through and completed that learning process? Many started, few finished.

I saw this interview with Charlie Sheen on one of those entertainment shows a couple of months back. He talked about how he planned to learn how to play an instrument or learn a new language during the pandemic. But, as he concluded, *"Nothing. I didn't do anything."* And, that's the case of many people in life. They have the desire, they have the idea, but they do not follow through.

Sometimes we interact with people who want to tell us how we should have lived our life. *"You should've done that. You should've followed through with that."* None of us what to hear that kind of stuff. We all know what we should've done but didn't.

For some, that what they didn't do becomes the definition of their life. They realize it and they allow it to control their thoughts. They allow regret to become the definition of their life. But, is that healthy?

We are all defined by what we did do and what we didn't do. The thing about what you didn't do is that you didn't do it. So, you can never truly know what your life would have been like if you did do it. Yes, you may have the idealized image of what your life would have been like if you had followed through. But, you will never truly know. At best, that is simply a projected fantasy.

So, what did you want to do that you didn't do? Is it possible for you to do it now? Are you still defined by the limitations of what kept you from doing it in the first place: both in the physical realm of reality and/or in your mind? Or, can you now do it? Mostly, do you choose to? Do you choose to take that step that you didn't take in the past and finally do that thing that You Should've?

What is the Price of Tears?

04/Oct/2021 03:45 PM

As we have lived through this Age of the Pandemic I believe it has caused us all to rethink life. Yes, yes, as always, there are those oblivious people who just don't give a shit and they pass through their life in a cloud of selfish oblivion. But, most of us are not like that. We think, we study, we learn, we try.

So much has changed and is still changing since this pandemic hit the world. I have spoken and written about the causation for this pandemic and my beliefs on the subject in the past, so I won't do it here. And, in fact, that is not even the point... We have all been struck by a life changing blow, some of us have been hit hard and hurt. But, just like all things life, others have used it to their own advantage.

I think to this news story that was broadcast last week here on L.A. TV. Many people lost their jobs due to the pandemic so they, the powers-that-be, had the great idea to not allow landlords to evict their tenants if they got behind in their rent. Great for the tenant. Free Rent. Very bad for the landlords. How can they pay their mortgage on the building?

Anyway, this one lady was speaking about how this one man, apparently an actor, just stopped paying his rent. On social media he bragged how he had shot ten or eleven commercials during the pandemic and he posted photos of his trips to Paris and other European destinations. All this while the building owner struggles to find a way to survive. How fucked up is that? He didn't have to pay rent, or maybe better put, he didn't choose to pay rent, *"So fuck it. Fuck the landlord. I got what I want. I'm living my best life. And, I'm getting free rent. I can use all my money to travel the world."* This, while the landlord cannot pay her mortgage. Not right. But, that is how some of the peoples of the world behave in these situations. How about you? How much do you take and never think about the impact that taking is having on someone else? How much do you take and never think about repayment?

There has been a lot of pain throughout this pandemic. And, for all you anti-vaxers out there, you are partially to blame. Did you get the measles vaccine when you were a kid? Like most of us, you probably did. Did you get the measles? Probably not. Yet, you believe bullshit stories, made up by WHO, and you don't get vaxed helping to allow this virus to mutate. Do you know how and why viruses mutate? Why don't you read up on that.

Think how many people in the world, in developing country, wish they could get the vaccine but can't. Yet, there are those where the vaccine is abundant and they are too selfish and too stubborn to take it. Get a clue!

For people like myself, who have lost close family members to this virus, we understand what this virus can do. Yet, there are those who won't get vaxed; helping, at least in part, in keeping this pandemic going and literally killing people. What do you think the karma for that is? What is the karma if you transmit this virus to someone and they get sick and/or die? What will your karma be? You anti-vaxer, you are at least in part to blame for this ongoing pandemic. But, do you own it? Do you care? Fuck any supposed side effects that may occur somewhere (maybe) down the lie. You are killing people. Maybe yourself. Freedom isn't free. Pay the price!

So many levels of life have been affected by this pandemic. And, though most of the businesses, that didn't go out of business, have reopened, all things are different.

For example, as least here in the U.S., a lot of people adopted pets during the pandemic. That was/is a good thing as these people gave those poor shelter animals, who may have been put to death, a new chance at life. They are people too! The problem is, now the veterinarians can't keep up with demand. An appointment with my vet is two months deep. And, for those clinics that don't require an appointment, there are lines of people waiting outside hoping to see a vet for their sick animal. It's really crazy.

One of my cats died around midnight on Saturday night because we couldn't get her in to see a vet. We had a new vet, (not the one who knew my cat), but one that we paid over two thousands dollars to, a week or two before, just to treat her. Of course, they didn't feel like coming into work on Saturday—take the money and run and all that... So, we could not get my cat the help she needed when we noticed her taking a turn for the worse. Maybe it was already too late, I don't know? But, at least my lady and myself could be there with her as she breathed her last breaths telling her we loved her. But, she is gone. So, I/we are obviously devastated. She was a great cat. She was with us for twelve years.

That's just one example... That's just me... How about you? How has this pandemic affected your life: both in a negative and possibly a positive way? You should really take the time to consciously chart this out. You may have some new and deep realization(s) by studying you, your life, and your life reactions in this *Age of the Pandemic.*

You know, in all life events—all life joys and all life catastrophes we can learn, we can become better people. Or, we can do like that renter did and is doing; not giving a shit about who he hurts as long as his life is okay—as long as he is getting free rent.

Some of us/many of us have paid a very high price due to this pandemic, while others have taken a free ride. It's what you do with what you are given that makes you the person you are and will define what you will encounter tomorrow.

So, what are you going to do today? Who are you going to help? We are still deep in this pandemic and it doesn't look like it is going to be over anytime soon. But, what you choose to do does not have to hurt someone else just so you can make your whatever better. You can choose to step outside of self-definitions and self-selfishness and get out there and try to make a positive difference.

When you only help yourself, you hurt someone else. Maybe it's time to stop only thinking about you.

*   *   *

02/Oct/2021 02:21 PM

How often do you pray for forgiveness?

How often do you ask for forgiveness?

How often do you think you need forgiveness?

How often do you try to repair and undo any hurt or damage you have created?

If you never do any of this, what does that say about the person you are?

You Have to Want it
02/Oct/2021 07:06 AM

Like I always say, you have to want it or it just isn't going to happen for you or matter to you. For example, if someone gave you a rare First Edition but you don't care about the subject or the author, that gift isn't going to mean anything to you. If someone gave you an expensive Swiss watch but you only check the time on your phone, the craftsmanship and the precision of that watch is not going to matter to you. If someone gave you a '58 Les Paul but you don't play guitar, you wouldn't know or care about the value of that guitar. It's like my lady says, *"A guitar is just a piece of wood with strings on it."* But, you give me that book, I would cherish it. If you gave me that watch, I would wear it. If you gave me that '58 Les Paul, I would make musical magic with. Again, you have to want it to want it.

People want things all the time. In fact, most people spend a good percentage of their life in fantasy. But, if you don't work towards getting that something then you will most likely never have it.

I taught the martial arts professionally for years. Every student who came through my doors went away with a skill set. As long as they wanted it, they tried and they trained, thus they became. But, that is a physical and mental sport. Though some would certainly do certain aspects of it better than others, all can find their own Best Self if they want it.

For the multitude of people who attempt to enter things like the film industry, it is almost impossible to embrace that dream that so many possess of stardom. But, if you are willing to alter your dream, accept less, you can Become. But, to Become anything, to get anything, you have to try, you have to want it.

I was sitting in the courtyard of a temple, enjoy a tea with this monk I know. This young woman walks by and he jokingly says, *"I wish that girl with the earrings would take me away from all this."* To describe the woman, she was youngish, had short hair, and had numerous earrings in each ear. For that moment, the monk wished for something else. We both smiled and continued our discussion about metaphysical matters and the drinking of tea.

After this, I did not see him for a time when I visited the temple. He had apparently been put in Lock Down. I never said anything about what he said and no one else was close enough to us to hear his statement so he must have reported himself. He wanted his monkshood more than he desired a life of the world and that girl. So, he took the penance and refocused his energy, alienating the world of desire for a time.

People want things all the time. As stated by the Buddha, certainly, *"Desire is the cause of suffering."* You want, you don't have, thus that not having becomes the definition of your life. But, does wanting and not having have to be your end point? Where is the magic in your pursuit?

Everybody wants something. The primary premise of this world is that it is based in desire. But, wanting does not have to be a cataclysmic event in your life. It does not have to be your End All. If you let it control you, then it controls you.

But, if you control it, then you control it. Just like the monk, you can have a momentary want, but it does not have to change the trajectory of your life.

The problem that most people have, in relation to their wanting, is that they let it control their life. They allow it to control their mind, thereby controlling their actions. People do all kinds of bad things to get what they want. They do it to others and they do it to themselves. But, those are people who are doing what they are doing based solely on desire without a clear perspective of their personal reality.

It was like when I was teaching the martial arts I had this one student who had been struck by a car when he was very young leaving him with physical and brain damage. Nice guy. Really enjoyed training. But, due to his condition, he could not do some of the physical movements to the level of someone who had not undergone his trauma. But, he knew it. He told me his whole story the moment he signed up. That did not stop him from training hard. He trained with all of his ability defined by the definition of his ability.

This is something that everyone needs to think about in the pursuit of what they/you want. You must define your parameters. You must know you strengths, your possibilities, and your limitations. You must not let your undefined, unattainable desires over power your reality. For if you do, your life will be defined by nothing more than agony brought about by your lack of fulfillment.

Know what you want. Work towards its obtainment, if that's what you want. But, know who you are and what you are. Define what you want by what you can have. It will make your life so much simpler and more fulfilling.

In Review of Life
01/Oct/2021 02:49 PM

I was cruising over to PetSmart today because I needed a new filter for my aquarium. The streets have become like *Mr. Toads Wild Ride.* It's crazy out there. Ever since the pandemic shut downs opened up, everybody only thinks of themselves—like they are the only one on the road and they drive like shit. It's really nuts.

Me, ever since I got my car totaled a week or two ago, by some guy jamming down the wrong side of the street to get to an open median where he could pass some of the traffic jam, I have become hyper-aware.

Interesting, the guy apparently didn't have any insurance, which is illegal, at least here in California. So, when my insurance company contacted him he said he was going to sue me. Sue me, for him hitting my car. Awl life… I'm glad I took the photos I did on the scene to prove the culprit in this manner. But, all of the any of this kind of life stuff does is to add to the unhappy-making. Get insurance people! Then, the powers-that-be can resolve it/anything among themselves.

Anyway, as I was driving I was listening to this rather long-winded interview on the NPR affiliate KCRW with this female author who had written a book about her life and her affair with this well-known crime novelist. She discussed that she left her husband for this guy and did all kinds of the whatever due to her bad childhood where she developed abandonment issues. All I could think was, *"Oh, boo hoo."* She grew up in a rich, famous family. She got caught shoplift in L.A. so they sent her to London where she got caught shoplifting again so then they sent her to one of the best boarding schools in the country where she had sex with a teacher and was kicked out.

Just a side note here... She sounds like she is around my age and the fact of the fact is, students having sex with teachers was not that uncommon when I was coming up. Anyway...

It made me think about how people react to the reaction. It made me think about how the only thing I ever stole in my life was a small meat cleaver from a super market, when I was about twelve years old, that I used to carry in my back pocket because where I grew up was so violent that I felt I needed it to aid in my protection. Again, we all have our reasons for doing what we do but when people do things that not only hurts the life and the livelihood of others but themselves for some bullshit, self-described psychological reasonings, all I can say is, *"Get a clue."*

You know, we all have our lives. We live them as best as we can. But, when people who come from wealth and circumstance complain it really brings out the critic in me. Believe me, if you look at my life and the lives of a number of my contemporaries who I grew up with, you would know what abandonment actually is. But, I don't let it define me. I don't blame it.

Listening to her speaking of the novelist got me to thinking about how many great movies were created via that man's writings. It got me to pondering how one of the movies that was based on a novel by this author got panned by some critics. Which led me to thinking, (once again), *"Who are these critics? Have they ever made a real film?"* And, to my longstanding statement, *"What is a film critics? With very few exceptions, it is someone who doesn't have the talent or the dedication to actually make a movie."*

Of course, I always need to state, that is except for Peter Bogdanovich. I mean, Bogdanovich is a GREAT filmmaker! He made some incredible films! Even some of his lesser-known works like *Saint Jack* and *They All Laughed* are hidden gems of cinema. For some reason he fell from grace from the industry. I don't know why? But, at least when he writes a review about a film he truly understands the entire process. This is a knowledge that most film critics do not possess.

All this started me to thinking about the fact of, if I were to critique a film, how would I go about it? I mean, I have been on all sides of the film industry both in the no and the high budget arenas. When I see a film I look for the lights; how it was lighted and where are the lights. I study the placement of the characters in association with background, the camera angles, the pans, the tilts, the zooms, the lenses used, the placement of focus, etc., etc., etc... And this is not coming from a place of ego on any level. It is just based on my experience.

When I see the reviews that most reviewers create, all they are doing is going over the most superficial and obvious elements of a film; they are just spouting out their ideas or opinions about what they like or don't like in a movie. But, what they are saying is not based in any true experiential knowledge of actual FILM MAKING. Sure, video is all the craze and has taken the filmmaking game by storm. And sure, I use it too. But, let's see you make a movie actually on film!

Just because you are a Video Maker does not make you a Film Maker.

That's why I and most other filmmakers state to the reviewers, *"Let's see what you can do."* But, they don't. All they can do is talk about someone else's work. That seems fairly indolent, don't you think?

The problem is, at best, most filmmakers are simply mimics. They do what they've seen done before. They write scripts that have already been written a hundred times before. There is no inspiration. There is nothing NEW, unique, artistic, or revolutionary.

To sidebar here: I was having lunch today at a little boutique pizzeria. There's this crazy guy who lives in my neighborhood. I believe he is of Korean decent. When you look at him you would swear he's homeless because his skin is dirty and his clothing are so old and so dirty. But, I believe he is just insane because if he were homeless I am certain the local constables would guide him out of the neighborhood. (There's medicine for that people!) Sometimes you'll see him on the street with his dick in his hand. No joke. Sometimes he pulls his dick out on the street. Why? Who knows?

Anyway, we had just begun to eat our pizzas on the patio of this restaurant. Up walks this guy and he plants himself right behind me. I mean, right behind my chair.

Now, I've talked about this in the past... Animals, children, and crazy people all seem to love me. Why? I don't know. But, we are still in a pandemic and this guys was standing just behind me. I blurt out, *"Are you fucking kidding me! Are you fucking kidding me!"* Then, I go into how this is the guy who pulls his dick out in public... I could just imagine him pulling his dick out while we were eating.

I'm told I can be a very intense person. Mostly, I don't mean to be but in this case I did. Finally, the guy took the hint and walked away and found a seat at a table several feet away from us where he pulls out a cell phone and lighted up a cigarette. Which is totally verboten in California—smoking in restaurants. Again, I get agitated. I was thinking of just getting up and leaving. Fuck the pizza.

Amazingly, this young, maybe sixteen year old, restaurant worker comes out and told the guy if he, *"Did that,"* he would have to leave. That was a ballsy move, I thought. I imagine they have had problems with this guy before.

The guy put out the cigarette and sat there playing with his cell phone, which may or may not actually be working, while I ate my lunch, with my lady, vowing to her to never go to that restaurant again. It was her idea...

You know, they have these new RayBan glasses that were just released this week that have a camera in them. I imagine you could get some great POV and natural footage if you had a pair of those. They're not even that expensive, like three hundred bucks. ...You could get footage of a homeless looking/crazy guy, dressed in rags, playing with his cell phone, with trendy people sitting around, staring at him and wondering what the fuck he is doing sitting at an outdoor table at this restaurant without ordering anything. That would make a great scene, I think. I wonder what the critics would say about that movie? They would probably critique the acting of the star player, (the crazy homeless looking guy), believe that his character was too contrived and that he did not dig deep enough into his character's development.

Welcome to Life...

*   *   *

01/Oct/2021 02:48 PM

There's no reason to fight when there's nothing worth fighting for.

*   *   *

01/Oct/2021 02:48 PM

If you don't get it done, it doesn't get done.

Then what?

*   *   *

01/Oct/2021 10:49 AM

If you lie about the truth what does the truth become?

* * *

01/Oct/2021 09:47 AM

If you set about on a path of getting revenge all your life is defined by is what someone else did to you.

*　　*　　*

01/Oct/2021 09:36 AM

Life is a slow process of realization.

If you're not looking for the new understandings you will never find them.

* * *

01/Oct/2021 09:33 AM

If you work everyday on making things just a little bit better before you know it everything will be better.

If All You Are Doing is Caring About Yourself Then All You Are Doing is Caring About Yourself

30/Sep/2021 05:10 PM

When you wake up in the morning what is your first thought? Does it involve you or is it focused on someone else?

When you go into a store, who are you thinking about? Why are you going in there? Are you thinking about what you want to buy or are you thinking about what you will buy for the greater whole of humanity—for people you do not even know?

When someone cuts you off as you drive or bumps into you as you are walking, do you blame them or do you blame yourself for being in the same space as they are?

Truly, how much do you think about yourself: your needs and your wants and how much do you think about someone/anyone else—particularly someone that you do not know?

If you look at yourself and if you are honest with yourself, most probably you will see that you think about you above all others. Yes/sure you think about that person you are infatuate with or in love with. You may even claim that you think about them and do things for them more than you. But, is that true? I don't know think so. All you are doing is doing something to buy their love. You are behaving in a manner that will make them love you—that will make them want to stay with you. So, your actions are about you, it is not about them.

When something negative happens, who do you blame? Most people blame the other person. It can't be your fault; right? Even if it is your fault, most people will do all they can to shift the blame onto the other person. They will lie and they will deny. Some are so blinded by their own self-involvement that they will not even admit the truth to themselves when something is, in fact, their fault. In the public eye, forget about it. The gloves are off and no action is too far out to be employed to win any meaningless battle.

But, why is this? Is this simply the human condition? Do you ever take the time to ponder how you interact with the world? Do you ever ask yourself who you think about first and why? Most people don't. They are very satisfied to focus on themselves and maybe even claim they help other people via donations and other giving. But, this is all a lie. What is giving? Isn't giving simply something that a specific person wants to do? What do they give? They give what they want to give. So, how is that a true act of selflessness in any way?

You can choose to not only think about yourself. The problem is, most people don't. Thus, what we are left with is a world full of selfish people, doing whatever they need to do to get over and get what they want. They take no personal responsibility for anything as long as they can keep the life focus on themselves.

It doesn't have to be this way but it is this way. But remember, all change begins with you. You can be a better, less self-involved person. But, will you?

In the Presence of Your Enemy

30/Sep/2021 10:12 AM

For those of you who know me, or have been reading me, (or for those of you just reading this now), you know I have been an aquarium enthusiast for... Well, pretty much forever... I have long focused on the freshwater fish of the African variety. Particularly Cichlids have been my primary focus through the years. The problem with Cichlid is, however, they tend to be very aggressive. The aquarium community will be fine for a time and then one day one decides to get all bad ass and starts killing his (or her) tank mates. More recently, my focus has shifted to African Leaf Fish. Of the same variety as Cichlids but far less aggressive. Thus, no murder.

So, that's all fine and good but then I added an Upside Down Catfish. A few months later, I added another. When they were small all was well with the world—their world. Now, they are like eight inches long and the one is a total bully over the other one. The smaller/newer one has to spend his (or her) life in hiding as the moment he (or she) reveals itself the other one goes on the attack. This has left me very perplexed as to what to do. And, it has been like this for a couple of years.

I actually bought the second one so the first one would have a friend. But, as many good intentions go, all it did was create havoc and chaos, especially for the life of the smaller fish.

I've had cats for the past three decades plus of my life. The first two I bought very close to the same time. They were kittens and they loved each other throughout their life. So much so that when one died many-many years later, the other one was so devastated she too die shorty there after. But, it hasn't always been like that. In some cases, some of my cats really disliked each other. But, there they were, they were put together and forced to live in the same space. Living in constant conflict and most probably unhappiness about having to be in cohabitation with that other Persian Cat.

I never had much of a family—being an only child and all. In fact, I really had no family, so I can't attest to exactly how this is. But, I have known some people who have brothers and sisters that they really hate. They really don't get along. But, there they are, (at least when they are young), they have to live in the same small space. What does this cause? I guess, a lot of very negative emotions and probably some dastardly deeds.

I know sometimes when people work in a specific environment they are forced to interact with people they don't really like. But, they need that paycheck, so what can they do? They have to, at least, play nice or simply avoid that other person as much as possible.

Why does life have to be like this? I guess, for many it is not. Some can simply separate from those they do not like—they can walk away. But, in other circumstances, like the case of my Upside Down Catfish, they are cast to living a life defined by the distasteful attacking actions of that someone else that they have no way to run away from.

From a philosophic perspective, one could argue that it is simply your self-perception, your projected-definition, your desire for people to be the way you want them to be that causes you to like or dislike anyone in the first place. Sure! That may be true. But, there are a lot of people who simply do not care what you feel, why you feel, or what their doing does to your life. Thus, if you are forces to interact or even live with them what are you left with? A life defined by conflict: internally, psychologically, and possibly even physically.

I can say, as most anyone would, leave those situations if you can. But, like my fish and some of the cases of my cats in the past, sometimes there is just no way out. Then what?

The only answer is, understand your definitions.

All of your life is a projection of your interpretation of this moment and/or that person. If you love hell it becomes heaven.

I used to play this mental game with girls that I would meet when I was young. Maybe I liked them, maybe I didn't, but I would turn this switch on, inside my brain, and I would decide to love them. I would actually allow My Self to feel that feeling of love. What I realized is that you can, if you choose to, actually turn that emotion of love on and off. Meaning, if you can turn that emotion on and off, you can turn any emotion on and off. Thus, even if you do not like the person you are forced to interact with, you can consciously choose to change the emotion you have towards them.

Now, this is not a technique for everybody. But, it is a technique that anyone can employee if they choose to.

You can decide how you feel about anyone. You do not have to let their actions and/or the who they are be the only defining factor in your love or your hate relationship.

So, next time you find yourself trapped with a person that you do not really like, instead of allowing that interaction to churn up all kinds of negative emotions in you, turn it around, take control, decide how you feel and make yourself feel the way you want to feel.

This may not ultimately change who a person is and what a person does but at least you will have the control over yourself to not let them be the only deciding factor for your life.

* * *

29/Sep/2021 04:51 PM

When you're young you think about all of the things you will accomplish.

When you're old you think about all of the things you haven't accomplished.

The Illusionary Self

29/Sep/2021 03:14 PM

The Illusionary Self... I could talk with you about his all day long. ...About how what you think you are almost never is what you truly are and what you think about: who, what, when, where, and why is almost universally false. It is all just a self-projected illusion.

All this is one of the core foundations of Hinduism and Buddhism.

I could talk to you about this subject but I generally don't because I want to bring people together. I hope to give them a new set of parameters on which they can rethink and rebuild a better Self. And, the fact of the matter is, most people do not care about this level of metaphysical mind stuff.

But, think about it, you and I live a completely different life in a completely different world. Even my friends who are out there reading this, though we may share similar interests, we are completely different people.

When you walk into a book store what section do you go to? That section may be very different from the section I would travel to. When you look out onto the cityscape, what do you see? What catches your eye? The things that you look for most probably are very different from what I look for. What catches my eye is most probably something you may never even see unless I point it out. We are each very different people and this is just one illustration of the illusion that people embrace each day of their life believing that they are different yet the same.

This is why I always caution people about attempting to understand or describe another individual. This is especially the case when they don't personally know that person. At best, all you are doing is judging them. And, what is judgment? It is simply you attempting to place your own life understandings and life definitions onto that individual. But, how can you do that? You don't them. You will never know. So, how can you pretend you understand them on any level?

Again, this is just another simply illustration of the illusion of life and how people fall prey to it.

Here's the fact, most people don't care about any of this. If they hear about it they will simply dismiss it. All this is something that they never even contemplate. All they think about is their life: what they think, what they want, what they feel, and what they must do on a daily basis. The mind of most people is constantly locked into a pattern of useless thought driven only by the life and the lifestyle they are living. They never attempt to rise themselves to any new level of understanding. They just think as they think as they think.

Again, the is another, more precise, illustration of how people fall prey to the Illusionary Self.

No one is better or worse than any other person in this world. Yes, there are people who do bad things: they hurt, they steal, and they lie. And, that's just a few of the most obvious crimes of a bad person. But, how a person thinks does not make them a bad person. What a person thinks about does not make them a bad person. Higher and Lower Self are simply a byproduct of the judging mind which, again, is simply an illustration of the Illusionary Self.

So, here's the question(s): How much do you think you know about life? How much do you think you know about you? How much do you think you know about me? How much do you think you know about anyone? What do you think about? Why do you think about it? And, perhaps more importantly, who controls your thoughts? Why do you believe what you believe?

When you look at life, what do you see? Do you see the projection of your own reality? Or, do you see through the illusion? Do you understand that life is nothing more that a process of you passing from birth to death based solely upon your desires and how you believe things to be?

If all you see is what you see, you do not see the illusion. If all you feel is what you feel, you do not take the time to understand your participation in the fact that what is occurring to your life and why it is occurring to your life is all due to your Life Projection. Your today occurs based on what you did yesterday. How you feel today is based upon what you have decided is good and what you have decided is bad. But, the fact of the fact is, all of this means nothing. It's just you projecting your Illusionary Self into your mind and onto the reality of all those you encounter.

Try seeing the illusion. Try stepping back from what you think is right and real. Try understanding that not everything you believe is true and you may find a new understanding that causes you to step away from your Illusionary Self if even for a moment.

Try it if you feel like it. You never know what you may find.

It's What You Do With What You Do

29/Sep/2021 10:11 AM

So, what do you do when you do it? And, why do you do it?

In life, we are each presented with life events. Some of these events are joyous and happy making, others are just the opposite. What do you do with them? And, why do you do it?

When good things and happiness comes your way, how do you react? What do you do with that gift?

When something negative happens to you, how do you react? What do you do with that circumstance?

If you look to the life of other people, if you study their reactions, the way they behave is how they behave. People change very little throughout their Life Time. For most, when good things happen they relish in that good. When bad things happen they lash out. But, is that the only way it can be—is that the only way you can be?

Think about a time when you received a gift that you really wanted. How did you react to that gift? Really think about it. How did that gift make you feel? What did it do for your life? Did possessing it bring you all that you believed it would bring to your life?

How about your reaction to the person who gave it to you? How did you react to them? What did you feel, what did you say, what did you do? Did you truly appreciate what they gave you or did you simply feel you deserved it?

Think about a time when you were expecting to receive something but you did not.

You thought you would get that something but that did not come to pass. Maybe you were given something else—something that you considered lessor. How did you react to that gift? Really think about it. How did that gift make you feel? How did you react to that lessor gift? And, how did you react to the person who gave you that lessor gift?

Now, turn this around. Think about a time when you gave someone a gift that you believed they wanted. How did you feel giving it to them? What did that giving make you feel? How did you feel about the way they reacted to that gift? How did you feel about the way that reacted to you? Did you actually give them what they wanted? Or, did you give them something that they considered a lessor gift? How did that giving alter your relationship?

Really think these things though and chart this out. It will provide you with a lot of insight into you and human behavior in general.

There's also the other side of this issue. Those times when you are deal a bad hand. Those times when something bad happens to you. Maybe it was the other person's fault. Maybe it was your fault. Maybe the fault lies somewhere in between. How do you act when something bad happens? How do you treat the other person or persons involved? Do you ever take any time to chart your reaction before you unleash those reactions or do you just do what you do, say what you say, and believe you have the right to do just that? Do you intentionally set out to hurt that other person? Or, do you possess the humility to forgive and to turn the other cheek?

The reason all of these questions must be acutely pondered by you is that life is an interactive process. Life is you receiving and giving. Life is you reacting to life events both good and bad. If you do not possess a clear understanding of the YOU that is YOU, if you do not hold a clear knowledge of what you will do when you will do it, all your life becomes is a reactive nothing. If you simply behave by liking what you like, not liking what you don't like, and behaving in a manner that is expressive of those very low level emotional outbursts, what does that make you? Answer: a person with no self control and no higher purpose.

We all receive gifts from time to time. Sometimes they are Some Thing other times they are far more abstract. We all encounter life events that we do not like. We all encounter people who do bad things and they are not very nice. But, all of your life ultimately boils down to what you do with what you do. In very life event you have the choice in how you will react. You can be the bigger, better, stronger, more actualized and enlightened individual or you can be the angered, hurtful, bully with no sense of greater purpose than fulfilling your own needs so you lash out.

Take some time, view your past life events. Chart out who and what you truly are and who and what you hope to be. Decide what you do with what you do. Ultimately, decided to be more than any momentary life event.

The Unknown
29/Sep/2021 07:04 AM

I have a couple of cats. One of my cats hurt herself. How she did that I have no idea. But, she did. The Vet put her in one of those cone things that animals wear around the neck protecting their head. She has to wear it for like a month. It is obviously freaking her out.

If you slip and fall and break your arm or something, the doctor is going to put you in a cast. Sure, you're not going to like it and it may annoy you. But, it is going to be explained to you. You are going to understand it. For a cat, you can talk and talk to them, trying to explain, but they will not, they cannot understand. For them, all that is happening is some strange thing is wrapped around their neck and going out over their head and it is really messing with their life, their lifestyle, and all that is known. What is being lived is being it experienced but it based in the unknown. They do not know why it is happening.

In life, in your life, how many times have you encountered some unexpected, unexplained life experience and you question, *"Why is this happening to me?"* You know that it happened. You experienced it. But, it came out of nowhere and you don't know why. All you are left with is dealing with the aftermath. What do you do then?

How Do You Pay Them Back?

28/Sep/2021 02:48 PM

I was just watching a presentation on BBC about how a large, beautiful, highly forested park has been put in and a large apartment structure has been constructed on the site where thousands of Jews were slaughter by the Nazis in the Ukraine. There are only a couple of people who survived that onslaught left alive. They were children at the time.

Nazis slaughtered Jews across Europe. Compared to the number that were left alive, only a small percentage survived.

For those of us with a conscience that style of behavior is disgusting. Yet, look at the Middle East today. Speak with many a Muslim, even those who live in the Western World, and they wish to erase Israel. Whenever I have interacted with and mentioned to the people I know of Muslim, Middle Eastern descent that I love Israel, a look of disgust comes over their face. Meaning, this style of genocidal behavior is not left to the past. It is very close at hand and could reoccur in a flash.

Look to what the Japanese did to Korea and the Koreans. Look to what the invading Europeans did to the Indigenous Americans. Look to the Slave Trade. Look to Pol Pot and his Khmer Rouge. Look to the recent genocide in Syria. Look to the Russian and the Uyghur. Look to the kid on the street corner who is attacked by a gang. Unconscionable behavior has been a corner stone of human reality but that does not make it right. How do we pay these people back? Really, how do we pay these people back?

Many people dismiss this behavior. They say it was all in the past or it is the problem of some other country, somewhere else in the world. *"I didn't do it, so why should I care?"* But, if you don't care, you don't care. If you don't care, you can set nothing right.

I always believed that paying tributes to the slain does not change their reality nor does it change the reality of those who loved them. Just like when they give some person an award posthumously. Sure, that is great to remember their contribution. But, they are not here to appreciate it. So, what is the point? Why didn't you give it to them when they were alive?

This being said, entire cultures have been attacked and there have been attempts to eliminate them. THIS IS WRONG! Every person is a human being. They may not be of your race, they may not be of your religion, they may not be the same color as your skin, but they are a person. You should never hate a person that you do not know simply because they are not of your racial or religious stock.

There is no really good answer as to how we can pay these people back. But, if we don't try than nothing is accomplished. At the least, what you need to do is to reach out a hand of friendship and of help to those who have been injured—and I mean anyone. This does not have to be a grand scale of genocidal injury. It can be helping anyone person-to-person. But, more than that, you need to be the person who hurts no one. You need to be the person that causes no pain. Because if you are causing any person any pain you are no different that someone who participated in a large-scale genocide.

The main thing we can do is help. Be pure in your mind and accept each person from each race, culture, and religion as a human being. Never judge them. Never judge anyone! Reach out as much as you can with that helping hand. Always make someone/anyone's anything better than when you first met them.

The better world all starts with you. What are you going to do to help?

*   *   *

28/Sep/2021 08:37 AM

People always make excuses for god.

Looking to the Future Past and Other People's Karma

28/Sep/2021 08:18 AM

I was having a joking little sit down over coffee with this sweet young thing of an actress/filmmaker friend of mine and we were discussing the past few years of life. Mostly, we were talking about pre-pandemic because now everybody's everything got fucked especially in terms of creativity in the realms of things like filmmaking. Anyway, she made a few jokes about this blog and asked me why didn't I just write an autobiography because so much of this blog is about the goings-on of my life. *"That would take all of the fun out of the moment,"* was my answer. But yeah, thinking about it, I guess someone could put together a fairly well researched biography of my life if they read all of the entries of this blog. ...I think I've been writing it since 2011.

For anyone who writes a blog or does a vlog or writes novels or poetry or does whatever creative whatever they will understand that it is a very personal experience. How personal you make it is up to you but as it is an expression of a specific level of consciousness. But, the good news, (or the bad news), depending on how you want to look at it is, very few people take this blog back to its beginning. Yes, I know some of you have been reading it since it's inception but for most, they pick it up here or there, maybe they read it for a day, a week, or maybe even month, it gives them some food for thought: they like it, they hate it, they think I'm right, they think I'm wrong, or whatever, and then they are gone. All good. Each person's choice is each person's choice. But, for those who actually care, this blog is all out there—all the entries are in book form. But, the mind of today seems to live only in the moment and the seeking out the What's Free. Why buy or pay for anything if you don't have to?

I was recently re-reading the final autobiography of Ram Dass, *Being Ram Dass,* that he composed shortly before he moved away from his physical life. It's interesting... It's interesting especial for those of us who know about his life; listened to him throughout the years and read his previous works. Ram Dass always told stories of his own life and his own life experiences. That was one of the things that drew me, (and many others), to him. That book tells many of the same stories that he had told before but it tells them from a slightly different perspective. It's new but it's also old. It's kind of like when Marguerite Duras rewrote her seminal book, The Lover, and recomposed the story as the, *The North China Lover.* Both incredible books. The same but different.

Sometimes one needs to rethink a life story through the perspective of time. Sometimes one comes to new conclusions and new realizations about something that happened way back in the way back when. And, with that new understanding comes a new interpretation of life events.

It's kind of like when people move on from relationships... Which was also something my friend and I were discussing. You know... I have known some people, mostly women, (but one man), who came from humble circumstances.

They got into a relationship; it ended. But, what they came away with was an entirely new and better life and/or lifestyle. They got to keep a grand house. Something they could never have personally afforded. They got a lot of money and in some cases an ongoing supply of money. They got pushed into a new life that was so much better than the life they originally came from. They got handed a new lifestyle simply because they were in a relationship for a time, it ended, and they got to keep what they got; earned and paid for by the other member of that relationship's money.

I wondered, as we were discussing, how many of those people actually give thanks to the person who gave them all of that? I would doubt that they do. When a relationship goes bad, they generally go very bad; and negativity is all that is felt. At least that is the words that are spoken by the people I know who have ended up on the other end of this equation. Yet, there that person is, living in a grand home, driving a nice car, being provided with a monthly allowance, simply because they could not keep their relationship together.

I don't know??? Something just seems wrong in all of that. It seems like that person who ends up with Life-Betterment, based on leaving a relationship, while forever taking from that other person, is on the wrong side of karma.

It's like all the people who get by taking. However they take is almost not even important. What is important is simply the fact that they do take. Think about life around you. Think about the people around you. How many people do you know who take something that was not given to them? Do you ever even question their actions? If you don't, you should. How about you, do you do that? What is the karma for that?

Then, there are all of these people out there, like me, who work to survive. But, what do the takers give to me? What do they give to us?

And, I'm just using me as an example. Talking goes on all over the place, all the time. But, when someone is getting something they want, by whatever means they are getting it, they never seem to care about the karma of their taking. They never give their taking any thought.

This is why I always feel it is so important for people to say something—say something when you see something going wrong. When someone is doing, saying, or writing something negative; intercede, stop them, and change the course of the conversation. Say or write something positive to countermand their actions. Make them realize that what they are doing, what they are saying is not right or righteous. Because silent is one of the most evil villains. Whether it is in Real Life, a conversation, on the internet, wherever… Meet that negativity with positivity. But again, people are willing to take but there are all of these excuses why they do not give. So, they do nothing.

The takers never like to hear that they are doing something wrong. They are getting what they want. Why should they care? But, they should be alerted to the fact that what they are doing is wrong. Who better to do that than you? Again, silent is one of the most evil villains. And, it lets people get away with a lot of bad doings.

I see the taking and the not giving all the time across the internet. If you don't see it, you're not looking. But again, most people don't want to know. Most people don't want to hear this. They just want to hear what they want to hear. They don't want to think about the karma of their actions. They don't want to think about what affect what they are doing is having on someone else.

I also have seen the giving. People give money to girls on the internet all the time; in all kinds of ways. Since the birth of the internet, it has been this way. Like I recently mentioned in this blog, men are based in this fantasy world and if they can hold a fantasy about a woman, if that woman provides them with something to fantasize about, then the wallet is open. But, that level of give and take is all based in illusion. And, all illusion leads to is eventual hurt.

The reason I bring all of this up is my friend, who as stated is young and I would say very pretty, gets all kinds of inappropriate stuff all the time sent her direction simply for the reason of taking. So much so that she has pulled back her internet presence. But again, it all goes to the taking and the not giving. It all goes to the creativity and artistry verses the unenlightened. It all goes to time: loving now and spanning back through the past. It all goes to caring about who you care about and what do you do for them? But, what do you give them? Do you only take what they have to give? Do you make excuses for your taking? Do you ever even contemplate the fact that you are taking? Or, do you care enough to give something in return?

Life is this complicated thing. It is completed because most people don't want to open their eyes and their minds and understand the truth. Life is interaction. Life is give but it should not only be take. Life is caring. Life is caring enough to care about the person you interact with and/or get something/anything from. So, give before you take give. Give, especially if you take or you get.

As for this blog... I don't charge a, *"Member's Only,"* price to get into the secret realms of this website to read this blog like some people do. It's available to the world. I don't have ads running all over this website like some people do. I just find those so distracting. Does anyone ever even click on those ads? I don't have a Patreon account. I'm not trying to be an Influencer and advertise and sell you stuff you don't want or need. I don't try to get people to pay for my Zen Films on GoFundMe, Indiegogo, or any other crowd-funding platform. But remember, this blog is not just this moment, all of the Scott Shaw Zen Blogs, throughout time and space, are out there. If you want to know what I knew then, if you want to know what I lived then—what I was thinking then and peer into all factors of my life and my history you can, just pick up a book.

Wow... That's a lot of stuff on a several subjects but it all goes back to the basis of my friend and my conversation. To begin where I started, life is a projected interpretation of your experiences. My experiences are present here (and via the blog books) based on this HERE or the Now of Then. You can find out about my life and my life interpretations of life if you want to.

Just like you can take if you want to—take but not give. But, if you take without giving what does that make you? Your life, your answer.

*   *   *

27/Sep/2021 09:33 AM

If you're rich you don't have to tell anyone you're rich.

If you're smart you don't have to tell anyone you're smart.

If you're beautiful you don't have to tell anyone you're beautiful.

If you're good you don't have to tell anyone you're good.

Because they would already know.

*   *   *

27/Sep/2021 07:48 AM

If you ponder the fact that more than likely this moment of your life is going to be entirely forgotten then what does this moment actually mean?

*   *   *

27/Sep/2021 07:13 AM

I have two clocks in my bedroom. The time on these clocks are both set via a satellite. When I initially set up the second clock I noticed that the time on it was four minutes different from the time on the other clock which caused me to question, *"Which one is right and which one is wrong?"* As time has moved along the difference in the time on these two clocks has continued to expand. Now, they are like ten minutes apart. This leads me question, *"I wonder if time is actually shifting?"*

The Subconscious Mind and the Projection of Your Reality

26/Sep/2021 08:12 AM

Ever since Sigmund Freud, Carl Jung, G.I. Gurdjieff, P.D. Ouspensky, Pamahansa Yogananada, Aleister Crowley, Abraham Harold Maslow, Norman Vincent Peals, onto all the little known or unknown philosophers and psychologists who have tried to paint a picture that there is a different reality out there and in that reality one may capture and harness what they want through their mind, people have been taught to believe that via their mind they can find a pathway to life fulfillment via the process of thought. But, just what is thought? And, how does it affect who and what you become and what you may or may not possess?

Certainly, we all realize that if you think about negative things; if you think about hurtful things, if your mind focuses on taking and hurting then the process of your life is going to be defined by those thoughts. This is the same if you think about positive and helpful things. If you try to find a pathway of being focused only the positive and the good, you will (hopefully) encounter that reality. But, virtually all, or a least most of, the people who focus on teaching techniques of the mind becoming a pathway to living the reality that you want to live never detail the reality of the other person. Meaning, not only is your life defined by what is on your mind but it is also defined by what is on the mind of that other person. Here is where many of the problem of life arise, especially in terms of Mind Science.

Ever since the dawning of the New Age, there has been countless people who have spoken and written about how you can project your thoughts to get what you want. They teach that if you focus your mind you can what you desire. Sure, if you seek you will find. If you are focusing on, looking for, and developing a pathway to get that abstract something, you may well get it. But, that is a Thing. That is not a Life.

Many teacher also claim that you can project your desires onto other people, as well. They teach that if you focus your mind on someone you can get that someone to do what you want them to do. But, for anyone who has tried this technique, you quickly come to realize that unless the person you are focusing your attentions upon is of a like mind, and wants the same things as you, it just ain't gonna happen.

But, more than that, why do you want that someone else to behave in the manner that you want them to behave in the first place? Why do you want them to do what you want them to do? On an even deeper level, what gives you the right to try to command them to do anything? Isn't that a very selfish framework from which to operate your life?

This is where all of the problems with Mind Science begin and, in fact, are put into practice. All of this Mind Stuff is focused on the Self. It is focused on one person either trying to get what they want or getting someone else to do what they want. Certainly, the practice of psychoanalysis and psychology cannot be condemned when it is focused on helping to correct the hurt mind of an individual. But, the reality of the reality is, people do not only base these practices on helping. Many attempt to use these tools, via redevelopment, to make them a something that one person can use against another person or perhaps even better put as a tool to get what one person wants from that other person.

Ask yourself, what do you want? Do you ask yourself that question each time you encounter a new person? Do you ask that question each time you encounter a person you already know?

The entire process of, *"Getting,"* is based on your, *"Wanting."* Because some people do not have what they want in their life—because they are not able to get it or achieve it by normal means, some seek out a pathway with promised techniques in order to obtain it. But, how selfish is that? You want what you want, you can't get it by normal means, so you seek out some psychological or magical spell in order to obtain it?

What all this boils down to is the fact that people who base their life upon the obtainment of their desires set about on a course that never takes the other person into consideration. They simply want what they want and seek out a method of its achievement. But, is that path ever defined by purity and or a god-conscience mindset? No. It is based in Self. And, only Self.

I could detail the fact that if you wish to follow a True Life Path then you should seek out a pathway that focuses on the immersive nothing of Life Reality via a school that does not focus solely on the Betterment of the Mind-Full YOU. A path that is not solely focused upon you getting what you want. But, how many people even care about that life and/or lifestyle? Look at all the people who claim spiritually out there. They too are full of Self and are on a pathway of getting what they want, even if what they want is supposedly based in some form of spirituality. But, is any pathway where one person comes to the forefront of getting what they want based on a pure and spiritual consciousness? Answer: No.

So, what does this leave us with? It leaves us with YOU. It leaves us with the YOU that interacts with the world. It leaves us with the YOU that wants what YOU want. It leaves us with what is the YOU who wants what YOU want and what YOU are willing to do to get it?

You can want. You can set about on a path of achievement focused on YOU. But, how much time do you spend thinking about how what YOU want is going to affect the life of someone/anyone else? If you don't think about this, who are YOU? What are YOU? Are you a person following a pathway to the Greater Good of Life and Humanity or are YOU only a selfish, unthinking/uncaring YOU?

You can make this world a better place via your desires. But, following a pathway that is only forced on YOU and YOU getting what YOU want is never that pathway.

The Definition of Your Life and the Projection of Your Reality

25/Sep/2021 07:31 AM

Have you ever bought one of those pieces of furniture that you had to put together from a store like Ikea or something. Sometimes the pieces are so precise that you have to get them in the exact spot that they were intended or they will not fit together?

Think about your life; how well do your pieces fit together? How well do you fit into your life? For some, life is very simply, they find their placement, they fit into it, and they move through it with little concern. For others, it is just the opposite. They do not/cannot find a place to place themselves where they meet that perfect fit. But, why is this? Is fit based upon where you are supposed to be or is it based upon where you relinquish control and simply allow yourself to exist?

Think about your own life. Truly take a moment. How well do you fit into it? If you do fit well into your life, why is that? What is the reasoning for your fit? Is it the fact that you were dealt a good hand of cards, where you got what you wanted? Or, is it due to the fact that you simply accepted your reality?

What about if you feel that you are not well suited for the life you find yourself living? Why is that? What is missing from your life that would allow you to thrive?

If you look across the globe, if you look back through time, there were and are a good percentage of the world's peoples, in fact most of the world's population, who live defined by very meager circumstances. Are they living their Best Life?

From the perspective of those who live in the developed world, where opportunities are abundant, one may question, how could that be? But, isn't all life defined by your perspective of that life? One person sees one thing the way they see it, while another individual views it from an entirely different perspective. Moreover, you only know what you know. If you don't know, you can never know.

This brings us back to the question of Life Fit. If you feel that you are well fitted to your life, how much time do you spend contemplating, *"Why?"* Sure, for those who have found success, they may relish in the possessions they own or the position that they have. On the other side of the coin, for those who have not achieved what they desired, they may constantly think about what they want but they do not have. Yes, many make all kinds of plans in their mind about what they would do if they did have what they wanted, living the life that they wished they lived. Like many, you may even set a course for that life attainment. You may work hard to get it. You may even lie, cheat, steal, and hurt others to move towards that dream. But, do you ever stop to contemplate that Life Fit is based mostly upon an acceptance of your reality rather than simply the pursuit of that illusive something?

Some people are designed to fit into a specific mold. Yet, they desire to be that Some Thing Else so they spend their time pursing that whatever. But, if you look to those who do achieve—if you look closely, there are many who never truly fit into the role they have achieved. They have simply forced themselves into a Life Place and from this they live an existence defined by conflict, chaos, and the constant need to prove themselves; ultimately leading to a life with no Peace or Suchness.

Predominately due to the internet, this modern world allows a lot of people, from all parts of the globe and the global reality, to raise themselves to the eye-line of the all and the everybody. It has provided opportunities that never existed before; especially in terms of chasing that Thing, that Persona, that is Out There. All that is good. But, that does not change the fact of fitting into your Life Fit. Yes, it may give birth to a million more desires. It may even give birth to a million more temporary celebrities. But, it does not/it cannot change the essence of who a person truly is. Fame and/or success does not necessarily equal a True You.

Moreover, if you can't achieve what you want to achieve doesn't that mean that you shouldn't have it? Doesn't that mean that it is not the True You?

So, who are you? What are you? Where do you fit? You can have all of the desires that you want. If you want to allow your entire life to be controlled by ever-evolving new desires, that is your choice. If you wish to have all kinds of delusions of grandeur, that is your choice, as well. But, if you wish to find the true fit in your life, then you must come into contact with that true inner you. Because no matter what you achieve in a world where you do not truly fit, it will all equal nothing if you cannot live a life defined by an embraced well-being and the knowledge about and the experience of you living a life where you truly are who and what you are in the place where you truly fit.

What Do You Do After It Is Done?
22/Sep/2021 07:31 AM

Life is an interplay of thoughts leading to action leading to what those actions create in the world around you. Life is any interplay of what you think, leading to what you do, leading to how what you do impacts the life of other people. But, how much thought do you put into the what you do? How much time do you spend analyzing the possible reactions to your action and how it will impact the life of those people that may be affected? Do you ever spend any time thinking about any of this or do you just do guided by whatever inner motivation you feel you are guided by?

The fact of this life is, most people do not contemplate their reality and how their reality has the potential to affect the all and the everything. All they think about is what they think about and they give very little, if any, thought to anything else. How about you? How much time do you spend analyzing how the impact of what you do may impact the life of someone/anyone else? Do you just do or do you think about what you do?

There is a great ancient text that I often recommend people read called, *Vicekachudamanai, The Crest Jewel of Discrimination,* written by the Hindu Sage, Adi Shankaracharya. You can find it online. The reason I recommend this book is that, first of all, it was written in a time, a place, based upon a religion and a culture when the mindset of humanity was framed much differently. That alone makes it interesting. But, beyond that, if you can take the time to read between the lines, which is at the essence of all true understanding, you can gain a framework to make you question your reality, your motivations for action, which may allow you come to understand your life from a new and more refined point of view.

Okay… But, how many of you are willing to do that? I imagine that the people who read this blog are, yes, much more willing to choose to expand their mind and find a new and better framework from which to operate from. But, is that you? Is that the person standing next to you? Is that the person down the street? Is that other person on-line who is focused on the whatever else?

You see, in life we all do what we do, motivated by whatever we are motivate by. But, how many people do anything from a framework of true consciousness? How many people do anything without the hope for some return? And, this is where all of the problems in life arise, which brings us to the point of the piece, what do you do after it is done?

We all do what we do. Most do what they do based simply upon their desire for a desired outcome or they don't really think it through at all. If you point this out to a person they will either justify their actions or make excuses for them. But, what does any of that equal? Answer: Unconscious selfishness. Yes, in any given moment, with any given action, what a person chooses to do may achieve the end result they desired but what about the anyone else, what about the anything else?

You see this all the time, people get an idea and based upon that idea they do what they do. But, they do what they do without any clear planning for the effects or the reactions. If they are satisfied with the results, all is well with their world. But, what about the person who is on the other end of their results? What about the people who are negatively affected? What about the world in general? If what one person does is only beneficial to them and/or those who like, love, or support them but it hurts someone/anyone else or something/anything else, then should that action have been performed? The answer is obvious but how many people ever take any of this into consideration?

So, let's get down to it... How often do you contemplate the reaction(s) to your actions(s)? How much do you think about this before you do? How much do you even care? Do you only care when you don't like what occurs to you due to what you have done? And/or do you ever even think about the feelings and/or the impact of what you have done to life of others; especially when the outcomes benefits you?

You see, most people live in an illusionary world. If nothing really big or bad happens to them, they think everything is okay. If something good happens to them, even better. The problem with this illusionary world is that there are other people in it; both the seen and the unseen. And, just because you do not see the negative reactions that you actions may have had on the life of someone else that does not make those actions any less impactful?

Do you ever think about any of this?

I think we have all been in those situations where someone has done something truly messed up that has hurt our life. Then, you feel. Then, you care. Then, you think about the impact of what someone else can do to your life.

Turn this around… You've done something really messed up to someone else… How much time did you spend undoing your doing? For most, the answer is very little if at all.

In many situations in life, you really need to take things to the personal level to truly understand the impact of action. For most, they can only understand when something is happening to them. This is not necessarily right; this is simply the way that it is. But, it doesn't have to be that way. You could be the one with discretion. You can be the one who analyses your actions. You could be the one who cares. You could be the one who cares enough about the feelings of that someone out there, that you do not and will never know, who may be impacted by what you are thinking about doing.

So, what are you going to do after it is done?

One Minute Later and a Kind Word is Always Better Than a Growl
21/Sep/2021 02:29 AM

If you think about the random/flash traumatic events that take place in your life, there is one thing that becomes very clear, if only you had left home one minute later then everything would have been different and you probably would not be living what you were forced to live. Those car accidents, if you had left home one minute later, you would not have been where you were and the two cars would not have collided. Those negative chance encounters with people, if you had left home one minute later, the two of you would never have crossed paths.

Of course, this goes towards positive events, as well. Had you not left when you left then that positive whatever would not have occurred. If you had left home one minute later then you would not have witnessed that beautiful butterfly, bumped into an old friend, watched some act of giving kindness of one person helping another, or met that special person who came into your life. But, you did leave when you left, and it did occur. So, negative or positive, much of your life comes to be defined by the moment that you choose to do anything and had you waited one minute more then that life event would not have occurred.

Much of, in fact the most of, my life was defined by this fact. And, I guess, this is where my understanding of this understanding first came into play.

As some of you know, I had a very serious motorcycle accident when I was twenty-one. It was a Sunday. I was actually in the process of moving from one apartment to another one in a nearby building but, as I tended to do, I got on my motorcycle and was headed to my mother's apartment in Hollywood to have Sunday dinner. BAM a car didn't see me, hit me, sent me flying through the air, fracturing my skull in numerous places, and broke, cut, tore, and messed up a whole lot of other areas of my body. They, the doctors, barely saved my life. But, I was never really the same. All this was all based upon when I left home. Had I left one minute later, the car would not have hit me. And, that was not the only time some car hit me on my motorcycle over the years. But, for sure, that was the most life changing.

This same, one minute later philosophy, came into play in my life last week. As I alluded to in this blog a few days ago, someone totaled my car. What happened is that I had come upon the first movie I had ever written. Yes, written… You know, *Zen Filmmaking* not using scripts and all… But, it was the first movie I wrote, directed, and acted in. I have not seen that film in over thirty years. So, I was heading over to a transfer house to move it to a format that is viewable by today's standards. If it's any good I'll put it up on YouTube. Anyway, there was this big traffic jam due to the fact that there was road construction up ahead. Like I say, you just can't get anywhere in L.A. anymore. I was sitting there stuck. This junky old pickup truck decided to jump the traffic line. He goes down the wrong side of the street heading for the open median to pass up the line of stuck cars. But, in doing so, he clips my car. SMASH, you know that terrible sound of metal on metal. He doesn't stop. He drives on. Fuck Me!

It wasn't that he hit me so hard but what happened was due to the angle of the impact, he literally ripped out my front wheel from its whatever. And, this being a front wheel drive car, it's gone...

It's sad, I really loved that car. Yeah, it's like eleven years old. But, it was in really good shape and ran really well. It was very reliable. Except for the fact that it probably needed a good vacuuming, as I tend to eat an Everything Bagel from Starbucks several mornings of the week... But, other than that... But now, it's gone. Sure, the insurance company will give me some money for it but, you know how it goes, it's never enough to actually replace the car. Plus, I have to deal with all the dealing with—tying to find another car and all that. All based upon the fact, that had I just left home one minute later everything would have been different. The crash would not have happened. Maybe that guy would have hit someone else but it would not have been me.

So, there I was, standing in the sun, waiting for a AAA tow truck. Of course, AAA messed up the call and I had to wait for an hour longer than they promised. What else is new???

Anyway, while most of the people were giving me a scowl as my car sat there in the lane blocking traffic. There was nothing I could do people! The car wouldn't move. But, this one guy, as he was passing by... He was one of those clean cut, nice guys. If I were to play in the world of stereotypes, I would call him, *"A good Christian man."* Anyway, he rolls down his window and exclaims, *"Are you okay? Is there anything I can do to help?"* I told him what happened. *"I'm so sorry to hear that. Are you sure I can't help?" "Nope, just waiting for AAA. But, thanks!"*

So, there's the other side of all this... Yes, all things happen defined by where you place yourself in life—when you decided to walk out of the door, but then there is what happens in the after effect—what you do with what you can do.

You can meet your trials and your tribulations with anger and frustration or you can accept that it was all based upon what it was based upon. But, more than all that, when you see someone else's something, defined by when they walked out the door, (one minute too soon or one minute too late), you can try to understand their dilemma and lend a smile and/or a helping hand. Truly, it really makes everyone 's everything just a little bit better.

No matter what happens to you, bad or good, it all ultimately becomes defined by how you react to it. No matter what happens to the everyone else, whether you know them or not, it is all defined by how you react to them. You can get pissed that someone ran into the car, so the car and the person are standing there lost in the abyss, waiting for the AAA tow truck. Or, you can smile, offer a helping hand, and try to make their anything/everything just a little bit better.

Life is defined by the minute that you walked out of your door. Then comes your decision how to handle that experience. So, what are you going to do when you should have left one minute later?

You Can Only Control the Things You Can Control

20/Sep/2021 08:25 AM

How many things upset you in the Out There? How many things do you see on the news, online, or see or hear in real life that causes you to get that feeling of dissatisfaction running through your veins? We all have those things. For each of us those things are different. But, it is what you do, based upon those feelings that will come to be the definition of your life.

The fact of the fact is, you can only control the things you can control. But, most people don't realize this. Most people don't understand this. They allow that negative emotion of intense dissatisfaction to take control over them. They allow those feelings to control their actions. Most never question why.

Think about something that upsets you or something that has recently upset you. Why did it upset you? Take a moment and really chart out the whole situation in your mind. What was it? Why was it? What happened? Who did what? Why did they do it? And, most importantly, how did it affect you?

Many people become upset at something that does not truly affect them. They see something or they hear something that is based in the Out There—something that truly has very little to do with them. Yet, they allow that SOME THING to take control over them. But, why?

If you truly analyze something that upsets you, particularly in the moment it is upsetting you, you may very well find that that SOME THING has very little to do with you. Yeah, you may not like it. Yeah, it may make you angry. Yeah, it may frustrate you. But, in actually, it does not actually affect your life. So, why let it control you?

Many people do many things based in their dissatisfaction in a SOME THING that has very little to do with them. But, the problem is, negativity only equals further negativity and negativity will only come to cause further negativity to come your direction.

Here's the thing... We all feel what we feel. Certain things, certain actions, taken by others, touch that place in us where we just don't like what they are doing. But, they are doing it. Why should you let their DOING take control over what you do? Because, if you allow them and their actions to take control over how you think, feel, and act then you have given them control over YOU. They become the controlling factor of YOU. Is that what you want? Do you want someone who does something that makes you angry to hold control over you?

People do all kinds of messed up things all the time. Some of them you witness and you do not like. But, if you wish to remain whole in yourself and maintain your control over yourself and not relinquish your control of YOU to them, then you just have to see what you see, hear what you hear, love it or hate it, but never let the actions of others take control over how you think, feel, or act because the fact of the fact is, no matter how much you allow the actions of someone else to control you, there will always be very little you can actually do to change anything and if you try to change it, your attempts may come back to hurt your own existence.

You can only control the things you can control.

*　　*　　*

20/Sep/2021 07:13 AM

How long does it take you to forgive?

*   *   *

18/Sep/2021 12:49 PM

How often do you say *Nothing* when you could say *Something?*

Selfless Service

18/Sep/2021 07:36 AM

In virtually all forms of advance spiritual practice it is taught that Selfless Service is one of the greatest goods. ...That giving is always better than taking. But, what exactly is Selfless Service? Selfless Service is you giving/you helping even when it takes away from your own life.

Here is where a lot of the confusion of Selfless Service arises. Many doctors, nurses, ministers, or teachers will believe that what they do/what they have to give is Selfless Service. But, it is not. Sure, what they are doing may be considered a, *"Higher Calling,"* but what they are doing is something that they want to do. What they are doing is something that they gain ego gratification from. What they are doing is something that they are, most probably, being paid for. Thus, it is not Selfless Service.

Selfless Service comes from a mindset of surrender. It comes from helping someone or something who needs help even when it will cost you something very big to give that help. Selfless Service is you turning off any sense of reward or desire or any hope of any compensation, on any level, and helping—doing for that person or persons, (that whatever), simply because they need your help—they need you to do what you can do.

Think about it, with this as the definition, throughout your life, how many times have you truly preformed Selfless Service? How many times have you turned off the YOU and did what needed to be done to help that someone or that something else; leaving behind all of your plans, no matter what it cost the what you thought was supposed to happen next? My guess is, you have done this very few times, if any, throughout your entire life.

The fact is, most people could care less about Selfless Service. They care about Self-full Service. They want what they want and if they go out of their way to help someone out they expect some sort of a reward—even if that reward is understood to be simply *Good Karma* coming their way.

Think about the times you have been helped in your life. It felt pretty good didn't it; those times when someone unexpectedly came to your aid? Now, think about a time when someone helped you in your life and you were very thankful but then you found out they expected something in return. I imagine that changed your entire perception of the experience and that individual.

Think about the last time something unexpected occurred and you dropped everything, gave up all of your plans, and truly came to the aid of that someone/something else. How many times in your life can you say that truly happened? Very few, I would imagine. This is the thing about Selfless Service, few people practice it. Fewer yet are willing to practice it. Most people simply remove them *"Less,"* from, *"Selfless,"* leaving only, *"Self."*

You cannot really plan to practice Selfless Service because when it is needed it will happen in an instant. What you can do is be willing to practice Selfless Service the moment it is needed.

You can be willing to turn the YOU off and be willing to truly give.

Selfless Service is not easy. But, think about how much better the entire world would be if it were more frequently practiced.

A better world beings with you. What are you going to do next?

*   *   *

17/Sep/2021 05:43 PM

When someone asks you, *"What do you do,"* how do you answer?

How you answer says a lot about who and what you truly are.

I Hate to Hear Children Cry

17/Sep/2021 09:14 AM

Whenever I hear a child crying it always makes me very sad. When a baby cries it is so much more primal. But, when a child is crying, they are actually crying about something. There is something that they need that they don't have. There is something that they want that they believe they really need. There is always a something. Though their parents may not think that they need it or may not be willing to give it to them, when a child cries there is a reason.

If you think back to your young childhood, think about the times that you were truly driven to tears. If you do, you will understand that there was a reason for those tears. Maybe now, years upon years later, you may be able to rationalize why your need(s) were not met but that does not change the level of true pain that you felt back then.

For most of us, as a child, we are trained not to cry when our needs are not being met. Like when my father used to hit me over something I did that he deemed inappropriate and I started to cry, *"If you cry I will give you something to cry about,"* would always be his statement. I was trained not to cry.

Then, there is all of the male machismo that is placed upon men. They are not supposed to cry. So, culture itself keeps one from expressing emotion.

But, a child, their tears comes from a very primordial space. It is so pure in its emotional expression. I don't understand why parents do not answer their child's need when they hear their child crying?

My neighbors have a couple of kids. You can tell that they are kids raised in the mindset of giving. They get what they want and need. I believe their parents are trying to provide them with a good life. Every now and then, however, I will hear one of those young children truly crying. It just makes me sad. Something must be very wrong in what is happening to them for them to cry with that intensity.

I have a nice and nephew… Well, I have a few, but there are two from one particular family-structure. They too are children that are being provided for. I don't know that I have ever seen either one of them truly cry. They are being taken care of. How great of a childhood is that?

For many of us, at least those of us who had a less than ideal childhood, we can think back to the intensity of our tears. There were those times when what took place really hurt. And, though we may have been told not to cry or we shouldn't be feeling the way we are feeling, that did not change the loss or the pain of what we were feeling. Those moments are what come to define our life.

When a child cries they are crying for a reason. If you're going to choose to be a parent, it's really important to give a child a life where they don't need to cry. If a child is crying, you really need to find a way to take those tears away.

The Placement of Your Priorities

16/Sep/2021 07:38 AM

In life, what do you commonly think about? For most, they think about what they are feeling in a particular moment, what they want, what they think about someone or something else, how can they get what or who they want, or maybe just a whole lot of random nothing. In life, the thought process is commonly pretty normal; you think the way you think and that is what you think about. Then, something unexpected happens. Maybe you get sick. Maybe you get in a car accident. Maybe you slip and hurt yourself. Maybe someone does some big something that really hurts you or makes you very angry. Whatever it is, something big happens and then all your thoughts are forced to think about that.

Think about it... Think about a time when everything you think changed all of sudden and your thoughts were forced to be thinking about something that you probably didn't want to be thinking about. We've all had those moments. What did you do when yours occurred?

Now, think about someone else's something—something when they were forced to think about something. Me, right now, I think about (I remember) this one girl who had gotten into a car accident. That always sucks. You are forced to deal with all of that stuff that you really don't want to deal with. Your thoughts and your emotions are forced to focus on a place that your mind would rather not be. Wouldn't you rather be thinking about that stuff you normally think about?

Anyway, the girl because she was a girl, and having somewhat of an internet presence, she put it out there that someone had smashed into her car, totaling it, so she needed a new car. She offered to do things like send people signed photos if they sent her some money. I sent her some money. Happy to do it. ...Nothing wrong with that. It was kind of like barter; I give you something for something you give me. For her, she may have known that her being who she was, she could gain some sort of... ...I'll use the word sympathy for a lack of a better term. So, she got money. And, that's great.

Her thought process was she needs something—money to buy a new car. She reached out to the world and the world responded. But, why?

For example, if someone ran into and totaled my car, (which actually recently happened), and I needed money, I seriously doubt if I put it out there to the world anyone would respond. How about you? If you put it out there, who, if anyone, would respond? The last time you were forced into thinking about Something Big in your life who else cared?

You see, there's this whole weird play of consciousness that people fall prey to and never truly analyze. Girls, particularly internet girls, have this vast advantage because they are locked into the realms of fantasy. ...Something that dominates the minds of most males. These men, (or sometimes women), see a passageway to some sort of undefined something with that seemly knowable person in the realms of cyberspace. But, no matter the reason their focus is drawn to a particular individual, it gives them something (more than the nothing) to think about. If they can help that person, even better. Then, they have a purpose.

But, think about this, we are all drawn to what and to whom we are drawn to, but why are we drawn to them? When you are drawn to a particular person, do you ever truly analyze the reason for your attraction—particularly in the case of someone you will most probably never meet in person and if you do it will only be on the most superficial of levels? Probably not. Why? Because the fantasy is the fantasy and in fantasy all realms of possibly are possible. It give you something to think about.

So, think about this… How much of your thoughts are based upon what is not cast to true reality? How much of your thoughts are based upon the possibilities only seen in your own mind? How much of what you do is based upon your thinking about the abstract compared to how much of what you think about is based upon hardened reality?

Again, this brings us back to the point, when something intense occurs that is what you think about. You are forced to think about it. But, most of life is not like that; though some people do seek out that intensity because then it provides them with a reason to truly feel. But, that's a wholly separate subject…

All that being whatever, your life is your life and your life is defined by what you think and why you think it. So, what do you think and why do you think it? Do you ever take the time to truly analyze this process within yourself. Most people don't. In fact, at best, most people lie to themselves about what they think and why they think it. But, if you do not know why you think what you think (even in moments of intensity) you cannot get down to the essence of who you truly are and why you are where you are in life.

Think about it...

*   *   *

13/Sep/2021 01:53 PM

You can't stay in the same place forever because if you stay in the same place forever you stay in the same place forever.

Talent in the Context of History
13/Sep/2021 01:38 PM

You know how every now and then you're driving along and a set of really good songs comes on the radio. That happened to me this AM. First was Ed Sheeran, *Bad Habits,* then Harry Styles, *Golden,* then Machine Gun Kelly, *My Ex's Best Friend,* and finally, Jonas Brothers and Marshmallow, *Leave Before You Love Me.* It got me to thinking about the new season of *American Horror Story, "Double Feature."* What's going on is that it revolves around this black pill that if people with talent take it they get super successful and if you just think you have talent and take it you loose all your hair and turn into this blood sucking vampire-style creatures. My lady jokes with me and tells me if I took it I would go bald and suck blood. Maybe she's right... ☺

But fame, fortune, and success is this illusive master. Like I have long said, some of the best guitar players I have known never became successful. ...And, I knew and was friends with some of the most well-known players, particularly of the 1980s. Just like in acting and filmmaking, it always seems to be more defined by luck than talent.

I was in Venice over the weekend and there is this one guy, (an old-guy), who sings pop songs on the boardwalk. A few months ago, when the homeless problem on the boardwalk had gotten totally out of control, before the sheriffs stepped in, there was this news footage of one of the homeless men just beating the crap out of that old guy. Now, I'm not saying what this guy sings is necessarily bad, (to each their own), but I can imagine if someone had to listen to it on and on and on—like if someone had their tent set up right by where he sings, it may get a bit nerve-racking. My lady made the comment as we walked past the singing minstrel; he would totally turn into a vampire if he took the pill.

For some reason, all this set me thinking back in time—at least back in time for me. ...You know, how one thought leads you to the next and the next and the next. I thought of this one guy that I had not thought of in years. He had this magnificent voice. It was pure opera. I met him through the Sufi Order and whenever we would sing or chant his voice just rose above all of the rest. Pure talent!

Now, this all goes to and can only be defined by the context of history. Back then, for those of us who walked the spiritual path, (and a lot of others), we all, (both men and women), let our hair grow, we didn't shave; all attempting to live a more natural/purer lifestyle. The guy, probably a decade or so older than, (I was only sixteen or maybe seventeen), had one of those grand beards and he just fit the part of what you would imagine of that era in time with long hair and a long beard.

There was this girl that came around what were then titled, *The Sufi Dances.* Beautiful young Jewish girl dressed as the era and the lifestyle dictated in long skirts, Birkenstocks, and the like. I had eyes for her and so did my friend. She was a couple of years old than I and she gave into the advances of that guy. I understood... He was totally in love with her.

His voice got him noticed by, *The Sufi Choir,* which was group of Sufis located on the East Coast that sang, recorded, and did performances based upon a modern interpretation of the spiritual tradition of Sufism. Though formed in San Francisco in 1969 under the tillage of Murshid Sam, they were by this point situated on the East Coast. Thus, he had to leave L.A. if he wanted to follow his dream. He invited the girl to go along but she refused. He left broken hearted.

Now, I could go into the story (stories) of how the girl then shifted her attentions to me. But, that has never been who I am. I hold friendships dear to my heart and I don't step over the line. But, that's a whole other issue. Eventually, the girl moved away from the order. As for the guy, *The Sufi Choir* disbanded a few years later—the times they were a-changing...

This brings me to the point—the entire question of true talent and what does it actually mean? The example was that guy; incredible singer. He sang but his songs were forgotten. *The Sufi Choir* disbanded. Plus, he lost the girl he loved based on his pursue of his talent. Just like all the great guitar players I have known who played their music to no one else's ears but their own. Was their talent any the less? But, what did it equal if no one else heard it?

So, what is talent? Is it only defined by someone who becomes successful based upon what they do? Or, is it something much deeper than all of that?

We all love to hear the music we love to hear. That great song comes on the radio and we turn it up. Somehow, someway the music of those people who are played on the radio got to embrace their talent, for however long their fame is appreciated. But, is that the only definition of talent? Fame? I don't know, maybe it is. You have to answer that for yourself.

As for me, I have known so many people that I have considered truly talented but most never rose to the public eye. On the other side of the isle, I have witnessed a lot of others who did become truly famous but it was/is hard to define their talent. Again, what does this tell us? What does this leave us with? I don't know? If there were such a pill, as described on *America Horror Story, Double Feature,* would you take it? Would you be willing to take that test as to whether or not you have, *"True Talent?"*

Me, a commercial came on the radio, so instead of waiting to see what would come up next, I clicked over to my phone and called up the band, *Khruangbin* via on demand. ...Thought I'd listen to a band I consider very talented that are a bit more esoteric.

Talent it is a complicated question...

*　　*　　*

13/Sep/2021 09:46 AM

There are many people who breed puppies and kittens to offer them for sale. Do you ever think about the fact that the mother of these puppies and kittens must truly miss their offspring when they are taken away from them?

The Dynamics of Confrontation Leading to the No-Win Scenario

13/Sep/2021 09:36 AM

Certainly, in the urban centers around the United States, and across the globe, there are way too many people living in way too small of a space. There are far too many rats in a cage for it to be a healthy environment. Yet, the urban centers continue to populate as the societies where these urban centers are housed find new ways to enclose more and more inhabitants into a too small of a space. It's really not a good thing. Too many people means too many people's overlapping problems leading to too many confrontations where no one is any longer allowed to emerge victorious. But, the bigger question is, (or at east should be), should there be a need a for a winner or a loser in the first place?

I was driving to have breakfast the other day. Within just a mile or so I had two situations where a confrontation could have easily followed. I was driving, in front of me was this white Cadillac SUV going very slow in the fast lane, apparently not aware or not caring about the anyone else. What else is new? He (or she) was driving in the fast lane. All of sudden they decide they want to turn right at the next street which was rapidly approaching. Across the lanes they attempt to go with no thought for anyone else. I guess this pissed off the driver of the car in front of me, also an SUV, who decided they wanted to get in their way to stop the progress of the Cadillac. But, to do this, they don't look, they totally cut me off, almost causing an accident. I honk. I think, *"Fucking asshole,"* but I move along towards my breakfast.

Just a few moments later, I am again driving towards my destination, when this car, driving parallel to me, in the next lane, decides to change lanes and starts to swerve into my lane. Had I not been aware and, luckily, as there was no car in the lane next to me, I swerve out of the way. Had I not they would have totally sideswiped me. I honk, yell a few choice words at them, and move along. They, I guess become afraid, or whatever, slowed way down and hung way back. It wasn't like I was going to take it any further. What would be the point? But, a lot of people would have taken it a lot farther. You see it on the news all the time, road rage leading to people getting shot.

In some states, here in the U.S. it is legal to carry guns. I guess, in those states a lot of people do carry a gun. But, why? Why are you so insecure that you need to carry a gun? I'm sure most would answer, *"As a means of my personal protection."* But, if you have gun, you can use a gun, and someone can easily die; based upon some small thing like a traffic incident.

Here in California, where carrying a gun is not legal, some people also carry guns. But, look at what that one guy did several months ago on the freeway. A woman flipped him off, he got pissed off, shot at her car, and killed her baby. No gun, no death.

People are out of control. Too many rats in a cage.

If you look to this situation that took place a few days ago, here in the L.A. area, you can witness the rage in people eyes? But, rage over what; to what end and for what ultimate purpose?

So... There is currently a re-call election going on here in California against the governor. The frontrunner Republican candidate was in Venice, doing what candidates do. This man is of African-American heritage. First what happened is that a woman on bicycle, wearing a gorilla mask, threw an egg at him. Personally, I found the symbolism in that very offensive. She missed and his security guards stepped in to protect the candidate. Right away steps up this white man with a shaved head, getting all in the face of this one security guard. You can tell he is one of those guys who has learned that if he gets all bold and scary and yells, he will may win a bout without ever fighting.

Plus, remember people, we are still in a pandemic; screaming in someone face can be a death sentence because I would highly doubt someone like that guy is vaccinated.

Anyway, the security guard pays little mind, but when he turns around the guy sucker punches him in the back of the head. It was a wild punch and did little, if any, damage. The security guard moved along.

Even more than that, I question why there was no police on the scene. They had to know this candidate was going to be there. And, Venice has long been noted for its violence and unruliness.

But, there are so many levels to this and the reason why the dynamics of confrontation leads to nothing good. What if that guy's sucker punch would have hurt or even knocked out the security guard and the attacker would have been arrested? He would have claimed all kinds of justifiable reasons for why he did what he did. But, all that he actually did was unleash violence proving that he was an out of control individual.

If, on the other hand, the security guard would have turned around and counterpunched the guy, possibly hurting and defeating him, then what? The guy would have played the victim card; sued the security guard and the political campaign. Meaning, you can't win, lose, or draw as all confrontations lead to a no-win scenario.

If you win, you have won—maybe you have defeated your opponent but then what is left? Hurt, anger, karma, all being directed at you; for which, you will someday pay the price. What if you lose? You are cast to a situation where you look for a rematch. In this world of today that usually means the legal system and suing someone. But, what if there was no confrontation at all? Wouldn't everything just be better? No one would be hurt. No damage would be done.

As I was driving home after breakfast, this young Latino male, in his customized car, decided to stop in the left turn only lane next to be. I'm guessing he was pretty high. He sticks his blunt out the window and is trying to clear off the ashes. He does this while all the cars behind him are lining up and beginning to honk as he is holding up their progress. They are getting angry. He is high and doesn't care. He looks at me, as I am right next to him. I look at him. And, just like most things life, it means nothing. He eventually drives on. There was no fights. And, everyone's life is allowed to move along until the next confrontation can be found.

In life, you can get mad if you want to get mad. If you want to get angry there is always something for you to be mad at. But, what does that make you? Answer: a person who is motivated and guided by the actions of someone else. It makes you someone who is not only controlled by the actions of others but one who has allowed the doings of others to guide what you do. Is that who you want to be? Are you your own person or are you someone who is so out of control of your Self that you look to the actions of others to guide you towards what you will feel and what you will do?

As in all things life, it's all your choice. But, one choice leads you towards darkness whereas the other choice leads you towards the light.

Bow Down to Me

10/Sep/2021 07:40 AM

It seems that recently I've been writing a lot about the martial arts and the various aspects; both mental and physical that come into play with its practice. I guess I need to begin this piece by stating; I have been formally involved with the martial for longer than most practitioners have been alive. Well over fifty years by this stage of my life. In fact, closer to sixty. As these years have passed on, many of my contemporaries have passed on. There are still a few practitioners I know, who are alive and who have been doing the marital arts for longer than I, but as each year passes by, their numbers get fewer and fewer. And, as I have so often said, most of the truly great practitioners I have known, their memory has been lost to the world forever. They were simple practitioners or instructors who practiced and/or operated their school in relative obscurity. But, think how many of their students learned life-long lessons from them that they practice to this day.

I guess this brings us to the point of this piece; as I have been involved with the martial arts for so long, I have encountered so many practitioners, from so many styles, that I have been allowed to not only see the trends in the evolving martial arts but witness or even fall prey to some of the obvious shortcomings.

Some would say that the martial arts are based in physical warfare and from this, this gives birth to the warrior mindset and, as such, some practitioners bring this to all levels of their life.

Maybe... But, the modern martial arts are not the formalized military. The modern martial arts are not defined by a regiment. There are not platoons. There are not soldiers sent to fight a specific battle guided by their superior officers. If you learn how to use a samurai sword in the martial arts, most probably you are not training to go and kill an enemy combatant. And, if you do, you are probably going to jail.

Again, the martial arts are not the military. There is no formal rank structure based upon the singular component of protecting one's country and the interests of that county across the globe. What there is are people, schools, and organizations that are set up to embellish a specific style and/or a specific teacher. From this—from the undefined and undisciplined mindset of many modern advanced practitioners, there has become this sense of a, *"Bow down to me,"* mentality. Practitioners work to gain rank. Practitioners train to win combat scenarios in the ring. Some work to become prominent organizational leaders. But, how many of them work on truly finding the pathway towards a higher self and humility?

Like I have long said, if you live your life based upon competition, just like in the movies based on the Old West, you may win a bout or two but you will always eventually encounter the gun fighter who is faster than you. But, what if you were not competing, who would gun you down?

As I have been involved in the martial arts for so many years, I constantly physically train and I am forever revising my mental understanding of practices, techniques, and situations in my mind. I imagine that is the case of most long-standing martial artists. But, where/why does ego come into play in any of this? The only reason ego is allowed to enter this process, at all, is due to the fact that someone wants to be seen as something more—someone wants to be something more than you.

When one begins training in the martial arts it is not uncommon that the student develops a sense of admiration for their instructor and what they can do that the student can not yet do. That's natural. As one's maturity in the martial arts continues to evolve, they come to appreciate those with truly good techniques. That too is natural. But, where is the necessity for ego in any of this? Why does criticism and the, *"I am more than you,"* mentality come into play? Why does the, *"Bow down to me,"* ideology come to be actualized? Answer: It is just ego.

In what ancient manuscript is it written that ego should be one of the primary components of the martial arts? In what ago-old text is it written that one should bow down to anyone who is a self-proclaimed whatever who has found some way to gain some rank from some organization that did not exist a decade or a century ago? Where is it written that a person's personal desire to be seen as a something, *"More,"* should become integrated into the true truth and understanding of the martial arts? Yet, this is what is going on all of the time. I say that the people who are following this path are missing the true point of the martial arts.

Think about it, if there were no rank in the martial arts then the only reason anyone would have a reason to practice would be for the betterment of their body and their mind. Practice would never be based upon ego. No one could ever expect to be respected simply because of their rank. With this, the martial arts could return to embracing their true essence and purpose.

Training to become, *"Better,"* (in anything), is one of the primary components in the evolution of anyone's life. But, there are very few professions, like the martial arts, where one is allow to command people to, *"Bow down to me,"* and get away with it.

As I have said so many times in so many places, the best martial arts I have known are the one's who are humble and silent. They teach courtesy and they teach respect in association with the physical and the mental techniques that are the cornerstone of the martial arts. They don't attack other practitioners. They don't claim to be better or more advanced than any other practitioner. They don't broadcast their accomplishment to the world. They simply live a simple life, teaching their chosen vocation. For isn't that the ultimate expression of a good and whole life? Isn't that the definition of a good and whole person? Isn't that the definition of a true martial artist?

Just think if all of the ego and condemnation was erased from the martial arts... Wouldn't everybody's everything become just a little bit better?

The martial art should be a pathway to physical and mental realization. It should not be a pathway to self-fulfilling ego stimulation.

Life is all based upon what path you choose and what you do with what is available to you. If you choose the martial arts as one of your primary pathway to the betterment of your life, then, as in all things good, whole, spiritual, and natural, that path should be free from ego. Even for you non-martial artists out there; think about it...

When the Past Comes Back to Haunt You

09/Sep/2021 10:08 AM

Back in the 1980s, I was living in this place in Hermosa Beach and I used to paint these very large (and I mean very large) paintings. I would staple gun the canvas to the walls and work. Then, I move to this smaller apartment right on the water in Redondo and I used an easel on my patio or I would work on this drafting table I had. Throughout that time period I had this (then) very cool yellow Sony AM/FM cassette player that I moved between locations to bring along my music when my stereo wasn't an option. Time went along and I began doing *The Roller Blade Seven* with Don Jackson. Our offices, at the Hollywood Center Building on Hollywood Blvd., needed some music so I brought along that cassette deck. Don really loved it as he was all into that late '80s military look. Somewhere along the line, I gave it to him. He literally used that deck until the very late stages of his life as his in-car cassette deck. He took it with him everywhere. He used to play me new finds and the music he liked on it all the time.

Today, I was doing a Low-Con transfer of one of his films. I'm going to upload it to YouTube as it never really sold or rented very well back in the days of the Video Tape. I don't think it even sold one DVD copy when I later released it in that new-fangled format. In fact, I black-n-whited it as the Hi-8 Analogue color just looked so bad to give the movie an air of somewhat of a something. Plus, the audio is scratchy as he used the on-board camera audio as his sound source.

Anyway… As I did a quick scan of the transfer this AM, I came upon a scene and there it was, that yellow Sony cassette deck. It was playing dance music for a couple of people to dance to in a scene. It made me smile, remembering the way back when…

So, think about this… Think about that Some Thing that you gave to that Some One…

Have you ever given something to someone that they cherish it for years to come? If you have, what is that/why is that? What did it mean to them and what did it mean to you by your giving it to them? Did they ever tell you how much they appreciate the gift? Or, did their gratitude remain silent?

Has someone ever given you something that you cherished for years? If they have, what is it? Why have you cherished it? What did it mean to you by getting it and what did it mean to them by giving it you? Did you ever tell them how much that gift meant to you? Or, did you just take it and run?

In life, we all give things to other people. Some/most of these gifts are giving because we have to. In other cases, we give something to someone because they really want it or, like in the case of that Sony cassette deck, they love that some thing.

How many of the gifts you have given have been truly appreciated? How many of the gifts you have given have been discarded and not cared about?

Giving is one of the greatest things you can do in life. Most of the gifts you give, however, probably don't find a loving home. But, does that change the act of giving?

It's a complicated question, leading to a complicated answer. You can give and that gift may be loved. You can give and that gift may not be appreciated. But, if you don't give, then no one gets and what does that leave life looking like?

Why don't you give a gift to someone today and watch the outcome. Maybe it will make their existence all kinds of better. Maybe it will be something that they will cherish for years to come.

Is This Your Awake Day?
08/Sep/2021 12:03 PM

For anyone who has ever had a cat as a life-partner. ...I don't really like to use the word, *"Pet,"* as that has so many connotations of dominance and ownership that aren't really true. ...At least not true for anyone who actually loves and respects those who live with them.

Anyway back to the subject... For anyone who has ever had a cat in their life. And, I guess I must preface this with stating an, *"Indoor Cat."* ...Don't let your cats roam outside people, all they do is get into trouble and live a much shorter life.

Again, back to the point... For anyone who has ever lived with a cat you know that they sleep a lot. Most days they spend a good percentage of it asleep. That's just who they are. But then, about once a week, they have their, *"Awake Day."* A day when, yes, they may nap a bit, but they are awake and doing what they do for most of that day.

I guess you have to be a cat psychologist/veterinarian or something like that to actually know why this is. But, that is how they are. They have an Awake Day.

How about you? How often do you have an Awake Day? How much of your time to you spend sleeping in a dream-state and how much of your time are you Wholly Present?

There is no right or wrong answer for this. ...To each their own and all that... But, think about it, how much of your time, per day, do you spend expanding your consciousness, taking it all in: viewing, studying, witnessing, growing and evolving?

For most, I think, they never even think about this. They just live their life to whatever degree they live their life; doing whatever it is they do. But, actually contemplate this, what if you became Hyper Aware all of the time, think how much more of the All and the Everything you would/could understand.

There's no real technique to make this happen. You simply have to make a choice. Do you want to make that choice? Do you want to become Super Awake? If you want to, you can. Then, the sky's the limit. Who knows what you will discover.

Wake up! Make this your Awake Day.

* * *

08/Sep/2021 10:04 AM

If you don’t document every day of your life then every day of your life goes by without documentation.

* * *

07/Sep/2021 02:12 PM

When was the last time you tried something different?

* * *

07/Sep/2021 08:38 AM

How much do you do without thinking about what your doing is doing to others?

Letting Go Verses Not Letting Go

07/Sep/2021 08:25 AM

There are moments in each of our lives that come to shape who we are. Maybe those moments only last for a second or a minute or two but they are events that cause us to feel and experience life in a very exaggerated fashion. Though those moments come to be very focused in our own mind, the person or persons we are experiencing them with my not feel the same way about them at all. To them, it was just a momentary life-happening; here and then gone. Though this may be the case to them, for us (for you) that lived situation comes to be something that your mind returns to and returns to for days, weeks, months, years, or even your entire lifetime.

Take a moment right now, think about one of those situations that occurred in your life, that continually comes to your mind. Maybe it was an event, maybe it was a conversation, maybe it was a fight, maybe it was a love; it can be anything—for each person these life moments are defined differently. Think about that thing. Bring it clearly into your mind. Was it a good moment? Was it a bad moment? Whatever it was, think about it and try to come to a conclusion as to why it has become something that your mind frequently returns to when you have lived so many other moments in your life.

In many psychological traditions, the soothsayer says to let go of all memories that do not help your life. Many religious teachers, influenced by these psychological schools of thought, echo this ideology. But, if you were not re-thinking and re-living that moment for some reason, known only to your inner mind, why would it continually come to your thinking mind? Again, grab one of these moments, bring it to mind, analyze it, and try to come to some understanding about why it continues to be relived in your mind and how that moment came to shape your life.

For many, these intense moments are based upon an exaggerated moment of feeling; be that feeling good or bad, happy or sad, ecstatic or embarrassing. But, think about this for a moment, the people who embrace these thoughts, and allow them to be rethought throughout their life, live a very common pattern of behavior. Be this pattern based upon goodness or badness, positivity or negativity; what they seek, whether knowingly or not, is what they seek. They continue to encounter the same type of life-situations, time after time, defined only by the difference of the person or the persons they are living that moment with.

For example, have you ever had someone get mad at you for something you've done—something you've done that you did not even realize you were doing anything wrong? You may possibly understand their anger once it was explained to you but their interpretation of that moment was not the way it played out in your mind. Or, have you ever had someone accuse you of some type of bad behavior but later you found out the person, doing the accusing, did the same thing to others or perhaps they did something even worse, based upon the same style of behavior they were accusing you of unleashing?

If you look to this person's life, you will find that they do this type of thing all the time. That is how they encounter relationships—that is how they interact with people—that is how they live their life. And, though they may deny this fact, that does not change the truth of the truth of what they are truly living. Meaning, what they accuse you of doing they have either personally instigated or they have lived those style of relationships many times in the past.

It's important to note that not all of the people who follow a common pattern of behavior do so based in negativity. Some do this based upon love. Some go from one relationship to another, as short-lived as some of those relationships may be, but they do this to encounter a specific feeling that will trigger a sensation that will cause them to hold a memory in place—a moment that they will relive and relive and relive in their mind's eye.

So, here's the thing... Each of us has moments that we have lived in our life that comes to our mind more frequently than others. In fact, most moments of our life are simply forgotten. But, the ones that do come to mind, come to mind for a reason. If you do not know what that reason is then you can never truly understand the lessons that could/should have been learned in that moment. So, the next time one of these recurring memories comes to mind, take the time to truly analyze that memory; figure out what you were feeling and why. Contemplate what lead you to living that moment. Analyze what part you had in creating that moment. Mostly, take the time to truly study that moment to the degree where you come to the deeper understanding of that moment and how it came to shape your life. From this, that memory may be allowed to fade into the realms of all of the other memories of your life, where you lived them, you can remember them if you want to, but they do not reemerge into your mind taking control of your thoughts and your emotions.

* * *

07/Sep/2021 07:10 AM

If your life was constantly being monitored what elements of your life would you have to hide?

*   *   *

07/Sep/2021 07:10 AM

If deception leads to your success what does your success actually mean?

Crimes That Are Never Punished

06/Sep/2021 08:20 AM

As we are coming up on the twentieth anniversary of the 911 attacks, where aircraft were flown into the Twin Towers of the World Trade Center of New York and the Pentagon, and the aftermath of those attacks, the networks have been showing some interesting features. CNN is running the 911 documentary that was created by two French filmmakers who were actually doing a documentary about a young New York City firefighter at the time and ended right at the center of the Twin Towers when they came down. HBO is showing the Spike Lee Joint on 911. Plus, the new film, *The Mauritanian,* starring Jodie Foster, Tahar Rahim, and Shailene Woodley, has just been released on Showtime. Combine this with the debacle that was unleashed by the Biden administration with the evacuation of U.S. citizens and allies from Afghanistan, (which was initially based on the 911 attacks), that has been on all the news channels, and one truly gets to view an exactingly profile of what happens to people's lives when bad things are done to good people.

Certainly, when the 911 attack occurred, I was glued to the TV. I watched live as the second tower was hit and, like those on the ground and those watching across the globe, I witnessed the hands of destruction in real time. Lives were lost and for what reason?

Watching the end to the war in Afghanistan on the news and the impact that took place on 911 and then to view a theatrical portrayal of events of the aftermath of 911 in, The

Mauritanian, one can truly witnesses the bad things that people do and what occurs from these actions. But, how many bad things are done where the person who did them received no punishment? Yes, the terrorists who flew planes into the World Trade Center and the Pentagon died along with the crew and the passengers on that flight. But, what punishment was that? They made a choice and were promised to enter a glorious heaven as a martyr. The crew and passengers made no such deal! Yeah, Osama bin Laden was eventually tracked down and killed but what punishment is a rapid death?

Then, you look to what the U.S. did to the prisoner, Mohamedou Ould Slahi, (and others) as portrayed in, *The Mauritanian,* and you see that even political entities that are purported to do the, *"Right Thing,"* are very vicious in their applications.

I had read the book, *Guantánamo Diary,* written by Mohamedou Ould Slahi, when it was first released. Then, like now, (watching the film loosely based on that book), I was ashamed at what the U.S. is capable of doing. What the Bush, Rumsfeld, and Cheney power structure did with their enhanced interrogations, that was nothing less than torture, was (or at least should be) below all that the United States stands for. This torture is what occurred to Mohamedou Ould Slahi and countless others at Gitmo and, at least to some degree, is still going on. Mohamedou Ould Slahi was held for many years without ever being able to see a judge, then, when he was found not guilty, the Obama administration fought his freedom for three years. WRONG!

When you watch the film, The Mauritanian, you see, in some small part, the way a gang attacks an individual. In this case, the gang was the U.S. military and its associates like the CIA. These attacks are always based in one person or a group knowing that they have the advantage over another person or persons. Meaning, it is never a fair fight. I saw this kind of activity all the time growing up. In some cases, a person who I thought was a friend, completely changed their stripes and went on the attack the moment they were with an undefeatable power structure. That's what the U.S. military did at Gitmo.

I mean, look around you... Who attacks who? Isn't it always the person with the advantage? Isn't it always the person who knows they can't be counter punched in self-defense? Meaning, the people who do this kind of stuff are cowards.

We all hated what occurred on 911. It was wrong! But, those who attacked possessed a belief that they were fighting back against an undefeatable bully. Isn't that what Gorilla Warfare is based upon? But, what they did, as wrong as it was, should not have been met with individualize torture focused on one person. How does that change anything? How does a gang attacking a defenseless (eventually proven innocent) person equal just punishment or the righting of a wrong on any level?

Today, we can look at the catastrophe taking place in Afghanistan, brought about the poor decisions of a bully-power and a Commander-in-Chief who did not stand up for what was right. People are being killing and their lives are being destroyed simply due to a president who wishes to wash his hands of a problem that he had a large part in creating. That's the problem with a position of power. They are in a position of power. They are a bully. They can do whatever they want. Even when what they want and what they command be done is wrong.

In the Spike Lee Joint on 911 you get to see a lot of people who stepped up to the plate and did the right thing. That is the right thing. Do the right thing. When someone needs help, help. Even when that help does nothing for you.

Just as what is right is right, what is wrong is wrong. A lot of people do a lot of wrong things and they get away with it while others, the small components in the extravaganza, get tortured.

A country is only a good as its worst doings. A religion is only as good as its worse doings. You are only as good as your worst doings. Do you support the bad? Do you turn and look away when the gang you are in is doing something bad? Or, do you stop the hurting and stand up for the right?

There are a lot of people who have done a lot of bad things throughout the history of humanity. But, it all begins with one person suggesting one thing and then the all-powerful gang following through with that idea.

All bad begins with one idea. All bad-doing begins with one person doing one bad thing. You can make a choice. You can stop the bad which then equals the good.

Good begins with you and it never involves attacking, hurting, or torturing someone who had nothing to do with anything.

* * *

03/Sep/2021 08:54 AM

Are you thinking about and living someone else's something or are you living your own?

Can You Remain Sane While Living with a Crazy Person?

03/Sep/2021 08:48 AM

It has long been noted that who you associate with will come to be a dominant factor in the things that you will do and where your life will end up. For this reason, people are often reminded that they should not hang out with a certain type of individual. In fact, there are many cases when people are told not to associate with a specific individual. Though this is the case, think about how many people end up hanging out with, being with, and even living with someone who is not of a positive or sound mind. How about you?

People come together for all kinds of reasons. Sometimes someone is attracted to another individual. Sometimes it is the, *"Bad Boy,"* or the *"Bad Girl,"* persona that draws a person in. Sometimes it is simply a fact a life; you have a family member or someone you must associate with and/or live with to make ends meet. Whatever the case, some people end up being in the company of another person or persons who is simply insane. They do crazy or bad things and then the person who is in their company comes to be influenced and under the control of their actions.

Think about your own life, have you ever associated with someone who did bad things? Do you do bad things? Think about your own life, have you ever associated with a person who is notably, *"Not Normal,"* and does things that are against the accepted ways of the world. How about you? Are you like that?

The fact is, we can all feel sympathy for people who have a mental illness. Some people seek out and receive the help they need to at least come to control this condition, while others do not. They are allowed to live a less than normal lifestyle oftentimes at least accepted, if not enabled, by the person or persons they are living with?

Again, how about you? Do you fit into this calculation on any level? And, if you do, are you honest with yourself about the role you play?

The thing is, the people we associate with come to be one of the most guiding factors in our life. Whether we hang out with a person intentionally or not is almost not even the defining factor. What is the defining factor is that they are in our life.

Take a moment and think this through. Think about someone who came into your life and sent you down a pathway that you later regretted or caused you to do something that you wish you had not done. Why did that happen? Answer: Because that person was in your life. If they were not then that, *"Whatever,"* would not have occurred.

Here's the thing, if you surround yourself with negative or mentally ill people that will come to be the definition of your life. Why? Because they will not only be the person who is causing you to do what you do but they will be the one causing you to feel a specific set of emotions that you would not be feeling if they were not in your life. Thus, they come to be the defining factor of your life.

Here's the question, *"Can you remain sane while living with a crazy person?"* The answer, *"No, you cannot."*

Whomever you surround yourself with comes to be the defining factor of your life, it is as simple as that. They will be the one who causes you to do what you do and feel what you feel. So, what are you going to do about this?

Most of us are not defined by living with a person who is dominated by mental instability. Most of us are not defined by living with a person who is dominated by hurtful negativity. But, there are a lot of people out there who are.

As in all cases, life is a choice we make. For the mentally ill, they can realize their condition and work to get the help they need or they cannot. Their choice. For those in association with that level of person, they can choose to be in association with them or not. Their choice.

Life is a choice. And, you do have to make a decision. You can be insane, you be in association with those who are insane, or you can be/become mentally healthy. What are you going to do? What style of life will you live? And, who are you going to choose to associate with?

Your life, your sanity...

*   *   *

02/Sep/2021 09:23 AM

What are you planning to do today about the negative words someone else has or is speaking?

What are you planning to do today about the negative words you have or are speaking?

If you don't do anything then nothing is done.

The Things That You Will Never Figure Out

02/Sep/2021 08:03 AM

Life is a pathway of realization based upon the fact that you will never be able to figure it all out. There are all of the things that you strive to know but many things will forever remain a mystery. Some people spend their entire lifetime attempting to find the answers. Others do not even care to try. But, no matter how or why you come at it, you will never know what you cannot know.

From the Hindu understanding of reality, all life is an illusion. It is all, *"Maya."* This philosophy has sent many down the road to peel back the layers of illusion in an attempt to find the truth. But, the reality of the reality is, the greatest illusion is that there is no illusion at all. What is, is and it is a simple as that. But, to arrive at this realization takes a lifetime of study.

The easiest way to take yourself to the place where you realize that you do not and you cannot know everything is simple, just contemplate something you do not understand. This can be some grand mathematic calculation or it can be something very simple. But, think about something that you do not understand. Now, try to find the pathway to its understanding. Here's the trick, most people never even try. They see what they see, they think they know what they think they know, but they never truly try to come to an absolute understanding of what they don't know. Why don't they know? What don't you know? What are you going to do about it?

Where I live, I can see this parking lot. Cars come and go all the time as they have done for years. Recently, there has been two cars meeting in the corner of this parking lot every early morning and every evening. There are two people in these cars: one man and one woman. I have jokingly labeled them, *"Part-time Lovers,"* referring the great Stevie Wonder song from the 1980s.

This couple arrives every AM and every PM. In the evening sometimes they bring fold out chairs and sit in front of their cars. Mostly, they just disappear into the one car, which is an SUV. My estimation is that they are both married and they find a way to pull away from their spouses in the morning and the evening. For, if they were a legitimate couple, why would they meet in the parking lot every morning and night? But, I don't know. I'm just guessing. And, though it is kind of fun for me to take notice of this couple and ponder why they are doing what they are doing; I will never truly know their reason why.

How much of life is like that? How much of your life is like that? How many things do you observe but you will never truly know the answer? Yes, you can speculate. Yes, you can think you know they answer. But, will you ever truly know the answer? No.

This is an ideal example of life; the part-time lovers. They are doing what they are doing. And, they do it religiously. They are doing what they are doing with an absolute pattern. It is observable. But, the answer to their, *"Why,"* is only known to them.

This is the truth of the truth. You can think you know. You can speculate about your knowing. You can even write a paper (like this) about your observation(s) but you will never truly know anything because all of life is unknowable except to the person or persons who are living what they are living and feeling what they are feeling.

Answer: There is none. You can never know what you do not know. You can spend your lifetime trying to find out an answer but, at the end of the game, the only realization you will come to is that you really did not know anything.

Think about it...

*   *   *

01/Sep/2021 11:38 AM

Is the world a better place because of your existence?

Mind Wipe
30/Aug/2021 09:44 AM

How often do you spend thinking? How often do you spend not thinking? For most, the answer is very simple, they think all the time.

Thinking has long been touted as the pathway to success—in however you define success. And, this is undoubtedly true; at least in the ways of the world. But, think how many people think too much. Their thinking drives them to emotional distress, anxiety, unhappiness, frustration, paranoia, and even mental breakdowns. Therefore, though thinking may be the pathway to accomplishment, it is also the road to mental pain.

Throughout history, particularly in the realms of Eastern understanding, turning off the mind has been propagated as an avenue to mental wellness. But, what is this process? For some, this pathway is prayer. For others, it is meditation. But, what occurs in both of these processes is that the mind is thinking. Yes, in prayer the thought process is directed towards God, (by however one defines that concept), for others who follow the realms of meditation, it involves doing things like reciting a mantra or observing the breath. But, are any of these techniques Not Thinking? No, they are simply a tool of replacing a single thought for the random thoughts that commonly exist in the mind of mankind. But, that is not, Not Thinking. Thus, though the mind may be conditioned to focus, these practices do not remove the process of thought from the mind.

In many spiritual traditions, the zealot is taught to sit down and pray or to meditate at a very specific time each day. For many, of this modern era, they do things like go to something like a yoga or a martial art class and then at the end of that class they are told to meditate. But, for most, whenever they try to turn off the thinking mind, they are met with the never-ending occurrence of the attack of random thoughts. Thus, they come to believe that they cannot truly turn off their mind. So, they no longer even try.

In truth, most people do not wish to follow the path of mental awareness. They want to think about the things of the world and the elements affecting their life. Most people, never even try to meditate and completely dismiss the process. Others feel it is for someone else but themselves. So, they make excuses. But, the fact of the fact is; yes, you can live your life without ever meditating but then all that occurs is that you have relinquished the power of your existence over to the All and the Everything that is Out There—to that whomever or whatever that forces their way into your mind by whatever means necessary. Thus, you have lived a life with no personal control.

As stated, formalized meditation is a process of causing the mind to think about one thing. Many find this hard. But, what about simply wiping the mind. Letting go of all thoughts, if even for a moment. This is much more doable and you may find it very freeing.

So… Here's the technique. Right now, as soon as you finish reading this, try this: close your eyes, embrace the darkness and the lack of light and simply wipe the thoughts from your mind. Don't think about it! Just do it.

What you will experience is a moment of divine thoughtlessness.

You many be able to do this technique for a few seconds or a few minutes. Each person is different. But, try it and you will certainly feel how freeing it.

If you want, once the thoughts come back to your mind, do it again; wipe the thoughts from your mind and feel the peace.

Mental Peace is out there if your desire to feel it. And, you don't have to do much to embrace it. Simply wipe your mind.

The Bad Things That People Do

28/Aug/2021 12:46 PM

I was sitting in the outdoor patio area of this local restaurant this morning having breakfast. I have a friend who owns a restaurant just across the street. Into his small parking lot this guy pulls his car into one of the only three parking spots, gets out, and walks across the street to the restaurant I'm eating at, where he goes inside and plants himself down with his laptop, planning to sit for who knows how long? He parked right in front of the sign, *"For customer parking only,"* without a thought. I gave him a cold hard stare as he walked by but what does any of that mean? I could see my friend setting up for his morning opening across the street, but missing one of his parking spot, which is very important to his business. All equaling, the bad things that people do.

Now, I get it, this is a very small issue among all of the larger bad things that are going on across the planet right now. And, when it comes right down to it, it is really none of my business. But, I like the guy—the restaurant owner. And, this pandemic has caused him to struggle just like so many other small business owners. But, here was that guy, not giving a fuck about anyone but himself and his getting a free parking spot. This, when there was a metered spot, on the street, right in front of where he parked.

Maybe it is that I don't operate from that Life Perspective. I really try to do the right thing. But, think about how many people don't. They just want to get what they want to get and they want to get it for free no matter who's life it messes up. How about you? Do you behave like that?

There was a part of me that wanted to say something to that guy. I thought about it... There was part of me that wanted to go across the street and tell my friend where the guy, who was parking in his lot could be found, so he could say something. But, he's a laid back guy. And, though he gets frustrated and angry, just like all of us, he probably wouldn't want the confrontation.

But, what that guy did was wrong. No matter how small of an issue it was. Wrong is wrong and that is that. If you do wrong you are doing wrong no matter what your motivation. You are hurting someone's something.

This is just something to think about as you pass through life. There is right and there is wrong. End of story. If you do something that is wrong, someone else gets negatively affected. Then, be prepared, because people will treat you the way you have treaded them.

It's Not All About You!
27/Aug/2021 11:42 AM

I had walked into this store today and entering just behind me was an African-American man who was not wearing a mask.

To place all of this is terms of time perspective, here in the Los Angeles area, masks are currently required for all indoor locations. For a time, the mask mandate was removed if you were vaccinated, but we are experiencing a large resurgence of COVID-19, via the Delta Variant, and, as such, masks are once again required. In fact, right now, more people are being hospitalized and dying in the U.S. since the early stages of the pandemic. So, the wearing of masks seems like a small price to pay to help keep everyone more healthy.

Anyway, I start to go about my shopping. The manager informs the man that a mask is required to shop in the store. He goes off. One thing leads to another… He claims to have a medical condition. The manger asks to see his medical documents. *"I don't need no fucking medical documents!"* On and on, he yells, *"What you are doing is illegal. Call the mother fucking police! I'll have YOU arrested. I have lawyers and I make a lot of money from assholes like you! I'm feeling threatened by you!"* It goes on and on and on… He was having a total Karen moment.

I've seen these situations on the news, since the onset of the pandemic, but I had never witnessed this level of confrontation in person. I thought to pull out my phone and record the altercation, but there is all this White-Black stuff going on right now and I didn't want to be the source of further controversy.

The manger was not letting up. She wanted him to put on a mask or leave the store. Had she been a small woman, I would have been more worried for her. But, she was big. I would guess about 6'2" and maybe two hundred pounds. She was, in fact, taller and bulkier then the man without a mask.

Finally, an African-American man, who was recording the situation, went up to talk to the guy and things seems to calm down. Me, I left the store. I hate confrontations.

Okay, but let's get down to the get down. Life is not all about you! Life is not all about the way that man chooses to behave! You MUST think about the other person!

This is one of the biggest problems that has occurred since the onset of the COVID-19 Pandemic. A lot of people only think about themselves. They don't want to get vaccinated. But, by not being vaccinated maybe you have the virus, do not even know you have it, but spread it someone who will become very sick and possible die from you giving it to them. If that occurred, who would be at fault for their death? YOU!

Just like that woman who intentionally coughed on that bus driver before there were mask mandates and vaccines. He died! That lady should have been prosecuted for murder!

Some people don't want to wear masks. I get it. They're not fun. But, right now, at least here in L.A., they are required. Why are they required? To help keep other people safe. Again, it's not all about you!

Just like the bodybuilder, actor, and politician, Arnold Schwarzenegger said in regard to the anti-mask, anti-vaxers who claimed their freedoms were being encroached upon, *"Screw your freedom. Because with freedom comes obligations and responsibilities."*

You know, this all goes to the bigger level of life. Do you only think about yourself? Do you only care about yourself? How much do you care about that person who may be shopping next to you that you will never even know?

If you don't care about them, where is your humanity? If you don't care about anyone/everyone else, where is your conscience? You really need to care about the other person!

The world is still engulfed in the COVID-19 Pandemic. But, if you don't take the necessary precautions, like wearing a mask and getting vaccinated, you are the one who keeps this pandemic flourishing.

I don't know, maybe this pandemic will bring about the end of the human race? It keeps altering and changing and people keep dying. But, no matter when you enter or when you exit your life, if you do not consciously care about the other person, (all other people), then all that makes you is a selfish individual. Is that who you are?

Life is not all about you!

THE ZEN

www.ingramcontent.com/pod-product-compliance
Lightning Source LLC
La Vergne TN
LVHW010054110826
845155LV00028B/330

* 9 7 8 1 9 4 9 2 5 1 4 5 6 *